ONLY ONE UNITED

Clive Hindle

©Clive Hindle – all rights reserved
No part of this book may be reproduced without author's permission
Published in London 2014

Cover Picture Credits:
Ryan Giggs: Pal2iyawit / Shutterstock.com
Cristian Ronaldo and Wes Brown Champions League Final held at Luzhniki Stadium Moscow 21 May 2008 and contested by Manchester United v Chelsea FC: Mitch Gunn / Shutterstock.com
Crowd: Jaggat Rashidi / Shutterstock.com
Champions League Final held at Luzhniki Stadium Moscow 21 May: Mitch Gunn / Shutterstock.com
Commemorative Stamp: catwalker / Shutterstock.com
Trinity: Debu55y / Shutterstock.com

All internal pictures from www.mirrorpix.com

This book is dedicated to Alex Hindle, companion of many memorable matches, and to fellow traveller John Warrington, now in NZ but still king of the North country.

About the Author:

Clive Hindle is a native Lancastrian who has supported Manchester United since he could first kick a ball. This is his personal history of the club from its early days to the Van Gaal era. The book places the club in the context of the English and European games over the years, including the present revolution brought about by the new owners in the English Premier League. His views are provocative and, in relation to the Glazer takeover and the club's rivals, often controversial.

This book is no mere football discography, this is not about a timeline of events, no, this is a passionate account with sharp observations and opinion that doesn't involve fences and sitting.

Old Trafford Stadium **credit - naipung / Shutterstock.com**

Contents

- CHAPTER 1 7
- THE FLIGHT OF THE PHOENIX 7
- CHAPTER 2 17
- DEATH IN THE AFTERNOON 17
- CHAPTER 3 25
- THE HOLY GRAIL 25
- CHAPTER 4 33
- TILTING AT WINDMILLS 33
- CHAPTER 5 41
- THE RELIGION 41
- CHAPTER 6 47
- THE HOME FRONT 47
- CHAPTER 7 59
- MEAN STREETS 59
- CHAPTER 8 71
- FOREIGN FIELDS 71
- CHAPTER 9 83
- THE CRUSADERS 83
- CHAPTER 10 93
- THE GLAMOUR GAME 93
- CHAPTER 11 107
- SEVEN YEARS IN TRAFFORD 107
- CHAPTER 12 119
- SCORCHED EARTH 119
- CHAPTER 13 131
- ROCK OF GIBRALTAR 131
- CHAPTER 14 147
- THE BANNER BRIGHT 147
- CHAPTER 15 157
- LE ROI EST MORT 157
- VIVE LE ROI 157

CHAPTER 16 167
REQUIEM OR REINCARNATION 167

ONLY ONE UNITED

CHAPTER 1

THE FLIGHT OF THE PHOENIX

The dust was still settling on the unpopular takeover of Manchester United Plc by the American business tycoon, Malcolm Glazer. I had just endured an ultimately disappointing trip to Cardiff to watch United comprehensively outplay a much vaunted Arsenal team in the England and Wales Cup Final and yet lose the FA Cup in a penalty shootout (the first ever in this competition). The fact that the losing penalty was missed by Paul Scholes, probably the most underrated midfielder ever to appear in the British Football Leagues and the real darling of the United fans for his modesty and the absence of a celebrity lifestyle, and that the winner was scored by Patrick Viera, a great player for France and Arsenal and a significant admirer of the Ginger Prince, made it all the more poignant and apparently inevitable. It did seem like the end of an era and it would have been difficult for even the most optimistic fan to see this period as the dawn of a new age of almost fantasy football.

The black symphony of the United fans[1], even in miserably inflicted defeat putting their Gunner counterparts to shame, was still ringing in my ears. Then my good friend John Warrington of Stockport, a town usually seen as a hotbed of Manchester City support even in those days before the Blue Moon's takeover by an Arabian crescent one, asked me the $64,000 question: did I see this day as a watershed?

I didn't have to ask him to explain what he meant. "Have you ever heard of the salamander fish?" I asked him.

"No," he replied, "but what has that to do with it?"

---

[1] Fans' group Shareholders United suggested United fans wear "funeral clothing" to "mourn" the Glazer takeover. Bloomberg 20th May 2005.

"Well," I said, "it's been around since the year dot and it's just about unkillable."

He looked around towards the directors' boxes. "Did it ever have this lot to deal with?" he asked.[2]

Many of us there that day feared that the Manchester United we know and love had finally overreached itself and was now locked into a spiral decline, which would not only see its fabulous achievements of the last fifteen years eclipsed by other clubs but might even condemn the club to oblivion. It didn't look good. Key components of the team were growing old and many pundits had expected Arsenal, in all but one respect a side of totally foreign talent, to win convincingly. Moreover, the Glazer family takeover had fostered such resentment among the United faithful that many called this Cup Final their swansong. They intended to make the ultimate sacrifice of not watching United again until its new owner had been sent packing. There was a degree of optimism among some elements that the boarders could be repelled because of a previous success. Unfortunately, on this occasion the MMC would not intervene and the supporters' associations were left like the Maginot Line, facing the wrong way, and suffering from near-paralysis in the wake of the Blitzkrieg.[3]

In more extreme incarnations a medium to long-term initiative was in place from an organised supporters' group to damage the club and therefore the Glazer family fortunes to such an extent that it would make the football club and its business "toxic" to any other buyer. It was hoped that the fans would obtain a significant shareholding. A group of fans had started up a new football club to be called FC United of Manchester, believing that this was the only way of preserving the heritage of the club. A lunatic fringe calling itself the Manchester Education Committee ('MEC') threatened mayhem,

---

2   It is a species which has been around since the continent of Pangaea existed 300 million years ago and it is notoriously difficult to dispose of. Individuals can enjoy life cycles of human dimensions.

3   IMUSA and MUST entertained such hopes because of the success with the previous Sky attempt at a takeover.

even murder.[4] Some thought that the acquisition of the club by a Jewish American would make it ever more vulnerable to the threat of terrorist attacks, a constant fear at Britain's large sporting venues since the horrific tragedy of 9/11 and particularly at Manchester United because of the club's high profile. Moreover, the corporate raiding nature of the acquisition, leveraged by American banks, meant that, after three years, when the smoke cleared and the mirrors were finally covered over, they stood there in their nakedness, as near bankrupt as one could get and still be standing. It had left a club, which prided itself on being just about the only financially solvent football club in the world, with a debt on its balance sheet of at least £276,000,000. Some newspaper pundits claimed, it seemed histrionically, that the debt was actually £800,000,000.[5] As another famous club, Leeds United, had gone into administration with debts a fraction of that sum it was small wonder that many walked away that dreary Cup Final day with as much rain in their hearts as there was in the leaden Cardiff skies.

Finally, the premiership duopoly enjoyed by Arsenal and Manchester United over the previous ten years (although in truth Arsenal had enjoyed two triumphs only and none back to back) had finally been broken by the new power in football. Chelsea F.C, a club more famous for its celebrity support than its success on the football field, stalked the arena, a gladiator bristling with arms. The armourer was a Russian billionaire, Roman Abramovich. It didn't much help either, for anyone with a sense of fair play, that he was not able to escape his reputation as a shady character, one of a so-called oligarchy of wealthy individuals who had profited from a corrupt government's fire sale of Russia's natural energy and other publicly-owned resources. The allegation was that he had deprived a whole people of their rightful wealth and condemned many to miserable existences. It was felt that Chelsea's gains were, in this way, ill-gotten and it seemed inappropriate somehow that the club's fans adopted this parvenu so enthusiastically. Well, of course they

---

4   The MEC's press release of 7th October 2004 threatened civil war of the football club (the supporters) against the company (the Plc) if it entertained the Glazer interest. Of course, at law, it had no choice. This was determined at the point of flotation.

5   The overall price was apparently just short of this sum. The fact that the debt stood at over £350m in 2014 suggests the higher figure was nearer the mark.

did. He promised (and delivered) success. So much of this detraction was sour grapes.[6]

Of course this was not of any concern to any Chelsea supporter. They basked in their good fortune (as City fans would a few years later) and they couldn't care less what people said about their slender heritage and former yo-yo-club reputation. They were the *loadsamoney* football generation and they were going to shake it up in a similar way to Real Madrid in Spain.[7]

John's was an interesting question but to my mind it began to form part of a greater one. I began to feel that, in order to answer his question properly, one had to understand how this club from the industrial heartland of England stole such a march on its contemporaries that, at the end of the last millennium, it was the wealthiest club in the world?[8] It had eclipsed its national rivals and forged ahead of the Italian giants, Juventus and AC Milan and even Spain's mightily successful Real Madrid and Catalonia's Barcelona.

This was an unlikely achievement and the galactic observer of football, if he had paused over the earth shortly after the Second World War, would not have expected it, particularly if the observer was privy to the fact that, only a few years before, the club had all but been bombed out of existence by the *Luftwaffe*. He would have been even more surprised if he had been told that, to heap tragedy on tragedy and irony on irony, as so often seems to be the case, the flower of Manchester was destroyed again on another German field in 1958.

The simple fact is, however, that the club's history is deceptive and relatively modest. Anyone looking through Lancastrian rose-tinted glasses may think the club was always at the top of the Christmas tree but, in fact, it was no stranger to reverses in fortune. It has faced bankruptcy more than once and in the 1930's it nearly lost Old

---

6   See e.g Martin Fricker of the Daily Mirror 5th November 2011
7   A character invented by Harry Enfield in the late 1980's.
8   Deloittes Money League. United dropped out of first place only in the season the club was acquired by the Glazers and at one stage (2005 – 2006) fell to fourth.

Trafford, a spectre which, for some at least, once again loomed large on that May Day of 2005. But instead of going down into oblivion it was that same era which saw the foundations laid of the modern club, the revolution having been instigated by a Manchester businessman, James Gibson. Supporters of the club who remember a time before the unprecedented success of the 1990's and the first few years of the new millennium are no strangers to a ride as good as anything Belle Vue had to offer.[9]

The culmination of all this was a night when it was good to be alive, one which will always live in the hearts and memories of United supporters. It happened on Wednesday 26th May 1999 when United won the League, FA Cup and European Champions' Cup, a historic treble, at least in the history of English football, and that is no mean qualification because the English league has always retained a greater element of competitiveness during a period when all football leagues have trended towards the hegemony of one or two clubs with the odd "incidental" contender.

Similar 'trebles' had been achieved in other leagues but the near-impossibility of the achievement in England's more widely-contested top flight, where football prides itself on the fact that even the bottom teams can beat the top ones on a good day, made it all the more worthwhile. Of course, the manner of the achievement helped as well. The ten men success against Arsenal in the semi-final of the F.A Cup, thanks to a goal from Ryan Giggs, which must rank among the greatest ever scored in the competition, was upstaged by the almost fairy-tale ending of the Champions' League Final in the cauldron of Barcelona's Nou Camp, all the better because United achieved this success without perhaps the greatest central midfield duo of their era in Scholes and Keane.

No one can forget that going into three minutes of injury time United was one goal down against Bayern Munich. This was a team which United fans may well have under-rated in the euphoria-building run up to the final, and perhaps the team did too because this was a

---

[9] In particular for me The Bobs, the wooden rollercoaster ride so called because the original cost of the ride was one shilling when it was acquired in the late 1920's from Fred Church of Buffalo USA. See manchesterhistory.net.

feature of the Ferguson teams at the time (and of Busby's a generation earlier[10]). Bayern's was a team highly skilled at shutting the door to an opponent's attack, as they had proved throughout the 90 minutes after scoring something of a fluke goal of their own, although the goal scorer, Mario Basler, wouldn't thank me for suggesting that the free kick which somehow got past an unsighted Peter Schmeichel was a fluke. It was a devastating goal for the red horde but only because no one could have any expectation of how this night would work out. United had acquired something of a reputation for failing at the final hurdle, having in the late 50's looked as if they might well win their first (and possibly more than one) European Cup only for Munich to intervene and having, in the mid to late 60's, threatened to win more than the one they won in 1968 only to fall short in 1966 and 1969. Indeed, because of the air-crash, the European Cup had come to be known as the Holy Grail.

Matt Busby and Bobby Charlton celebrate The Holy Grail (1968)

---

10 For instance, the United team of 1966, which was probably better than that of 1968 in that Best, Law and Charlton were all at their peak, beat Benfica 5 - 1 away but succumbed to the total unknowns of Partizan Belgrade in the semi-finals.

As I will revert a number of times to this description of the European Cup or, in its present incarnation, the European Champions League, I would like to make it clear now that I do not use it to demean the efforts of other clubs which have won the trophy, including that select few which have won it more times than United, but I mean that the tragedy of Munich added to the competition a poignancy which no other club and its fans could fully appreciate and made its attainment (and its continuing attainment) into a quest which carries the sort of Romance of the ancient Celtic myths of chivalry and is, to me at least, a sort of restatement of those myths for modern times.

The same pattern of falling short of the pinnacle emerged in the 90's[11] even after the club had forced its way back up the pecking order following two decades away from the top table. Even Sir Alex's teams suffered from this apparent failure of confidence. The 1994 team was hampered by foreign player restrictions and the class of 92 was perhaps too young until the 1999 triumph but one still had that feeling of a bridge too far and it persisted into the 2000's, particularly against traditional rivals such as Real Madrid (2000 and 2003), Barcelona (2009 and 2011) and AC Milan (2005) but it happened also against Bayern in 2001, Leverkusen in 2002 and Porto in 2004, all teams which one would have expected the United of the time to beat in a big match. Ferguson never totally overcame that feeling of inferiority against some of the top teams and top managers and the complex may have rested partially with him, although I doubt he would ever entertain the idea of his own fallibility.

Depressingly, after immense expectations, even that night in 1999 had begun to look like a match too far too, another glorious failure. But then the whole dynamic changed: two goals inspired by the dead(ly) balls of David Beckham saw United steal the European Cup from their rivals at a point when the maroon and blue ribbons of Bayern had already been tied on to the trophy.[12]

---

11   The semi-final against Dortmund in 1997 stands out; and later the semi-final against Leverkusen in 2002.
12   Wikipedia from various sources.

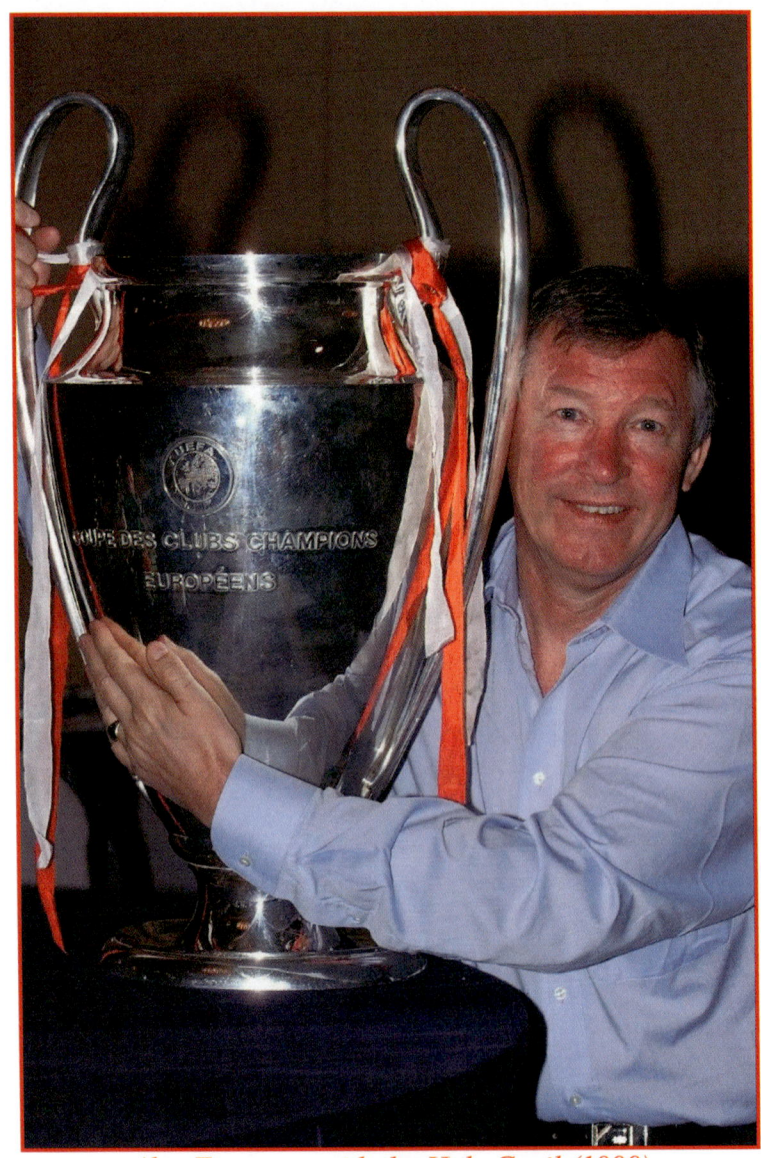

Alex Ferguson with the Holy Grail (1999)

In scaling these heights Manchester United stood pre-eminent in the game at the pinnacle of a century in which football had made the transition from a working class pastime, ridiculed and vulgarised by the upper and middle classes alike, to Pele's "beautiful game". In the

English game at least there have been few other teams whose manner of play would have merited that description. The history of the club is one of the continuing themes of tragedy: the cycle of birth, death and rebirth. That resilience is the point. This is the phoenix club, the team that took off into the dark, dark night, just like the Titanic, and died. Only the good ship Titanic – God bless her and all who sailed in her - could not rise alert and alive from her cold, watery grave. Manchester United, football's own Titanic, rose from the wreckage of a Munich runway and took flight. This is at the heart of the phenomenon that is Manchester United. But is it the real driving force of the legend?

One would be tempted to answer yes, except of course that, for some fans, Munich is not a relevant consideration nowadays and for many detractors it is a source of mischief-making. It is clearly part of the cause but not the only one and it is difficult to divorce the accident itself from the team it killed. The latter's fame was already assured. It is more likely therefore to be the incipient but already enduring reputation of the Busby Babes rather than the accident itself which is the genesis of the current fame of the club but that by itself would scarcely have been enough. There have been many great teams throughout history. The accident and the fact that it occurred on the great European adventure was the trigger for the release of the emotion which created the time capsule dug up for the first time at Wembley in May 1968 and then buried again until the final in the Nou Camp in May 1999 and yet again until Moscow in May 2008.

CHAPTER 2
DEATH IN THE AFTERNOON

Of that 1999 Champions League Final against Bayern Munich, with the Germans 1–0 up and seemingly coasting, unlucky even not to be further ahead as Schmeichel was forced to make two remarkable saves and they hit the woodwork twice, it is hard to forget the image of "Super" Mario Basler winding up the crowd at every corner or set piece to get them to roar his team home, or to further demoralise the United fans who had thought this their year. Unforgettable also was the strident German loudspeaker system which, even in a foreign ground, was, with typically forthright Germanic pride, ten times louder than anyone else's. They knew nothing of understatement, these guys.

I wonder, though, if any of those boys who plundered the European trophy from the great German's club's prematurely celebrating clutches gave any thought to the irony of the opposition's identity, or even had any sense of the mission they were on. Most of them had come through the United youth ranks or had joined the team whilst relatively young, just like their predecessors in the halcyon days of 1968 when this elusive prize first came within the club's grasp. The class of 1968, many of whom came from the youth teams stretching back a decade or so earlier, was already in terminal decline and its members knew precisely how lucky they were to hold up the fabled trophy. Bobby Charlton and Bill Foulkes had the most poignant memories. Etched on their brains was the remembrance of the cruellest day, 6th February 1958, when a bird failed to fly and a legend took wing.

The youngsters of the 1999 class won't have given much thought to the club's tragic history in this competition but I would be equally surprised if they were entirely untouched by it. Even in the oral tradition of football, which passes on from generation to generation, the tribal inheritance of the team, the past is a foreign country. Of one thing, however, there is little doubt: the pursuit of this aesthetically unattractive trophy is ingrained in the heart of anyone who plays for United. It has become an abiding passion, the ultimate goal. Those who tilt for it and fail are condemned to wander forever in a sort of neo-classical hell, unable to push a boulder up a hill without it falling back down again,[13] or to stand in a pool of water which recedes every time he stoops to drink,[14] forever bemoaning the incompleteness of their souls. Whereas those who stand on the pinnacle are at one with themselves and the world.

This magnificent obsession has made many football pundits and journalists refer to the pursuit of the Champions' Cup as Manchester United's 'Holy Grail'.[15] Two legendary managers, Matt Busby and Alex Ferguson, both working class Glaswegians, both knighted for their services to football and to Manchester United in particular, are, presumably, in the context of that metaphorical Arthurian struggle, the embodiment of Merlin.[16] Their legendary players are the equivalent of King Arthur and the Knights of the Round Table. In Sir Matt's case, it took a rebellion against the English football establishment to get his team into the competition and in that rebellion and the reason for it can be seen for the first time the beginning of the phenomenon that is Manchester United. Why or how, in retrospect, Manchester United seems to have stepped, like Mallory and Irving, from the ridge of history into the mists of legend,[17] is most easily summed up in the one word 'Munich'. However, although that is probably nothing but the truth it is perhaps not the whole truth.

The story of the last few hours of the 'Busby Babes'[18] has been

---

13   Sisyphus
14   Tantalus
15   The phrase appears to stem from the programme for the first division match between Manchester united and Wolves on 8th February 1958. The match was of course postponed.
16   Merlin is, according to some sources, buried by the Powsail Burn on the Tweed. There is a prophecy that, should the Powsail and the Tweed ever meet, England and Scotland will be ruled by one monarch. In fulfilment of the prophecy or perhaps merely ironically it did burst its banks when James VI was crowned James 1 and gave birth to a doomed line.
17   Both disappeared on Everest in 1924. George Mallory's frozen remains were discovered on 1st May 1999. Irvine's have not yet been found. No one knows if they reached the summit.
18   Frank Nicklin of the Manchester Evening Chronicle is usually given credit for coining the phrase as early as 1951 but it is not known if it was then in writing.

retold many times, not least in the words of some of the survivors of that calamity such as Harry Gregg, Bill Foulkes and Bobby Charlton. There had been omens, it appears, in the disappearance of Johnny Berry's travel documents in Belgrade, which delayed the flight to its refuelling stopover in Munich. Even before that there had been the opposition of the FA and Football League to the club having any dealings with Johnny Foreigner. United had better be back for the game against Wolves, one of their most dangerous domestic rivals, the following Saturday, or else. There was no Sky television in those days to rearrange the fixtures to suit the global audience.

The chartered Elizabethan aeroplane carrying the team finally left Yugoslavia in good flying conditions but one country's swallow doesn't always make for summer elsewhere and, when the flight entered Southern Germany, the wintry clouds were already closing in. Later, idling away the time in the Munich airport lounge, Roger Byrne was to notice the way the snow had covered the tyre tracks of the plane within less than an hour of its landing. It is a matter of record that the plane was in the holding area waiting for flight clearance when at 2.19 p.m. the tower gave instructions to taxi on to the runway. The next omen was that, accelerating half way down the runway and probably just short of rotation, the pilot aborted the take off because he had noticed a 'boost surge', a problem not uncommon with turbo prop planes at higher altitude airports. Returning to the start point the plane tried again, only to suffer the same problem. Anyone, even in this day and age of popular air travel, will have no doubt about the anxieties those young men must at that point have been suffering. They may have been gods and heroes on the football field but, the business done, basically, they were just a bunch of young lads on the hoy. This was suddenly no jaunt. Returning to the airport lounge this time, they will have bantered with each other to keep their spirits high but I am sure the cold hand of dread must have gripped even hearts of solid oak. Why did they not decide after that second aborted take-off to stay overnight in Munich? Well the answer lies in life's sequence of missed opportunities, its what ifs. What difference do they make if your number's up? If the fatalists have their way? The team was certainly offered the option of an overnight stop to re-balance the engines and eliminate the perceived problem. However, it was the received wisdom at the time that the problem would not have been fatal to the flight anyway. The precautions were purely that, a matter of dotting i's and crossing t's. The plane could function on one engine if necessary. A group of young lads who'd just witnessed at first hand the deprived lives of the people who lived behind the Iron Curtain, some of whom, even in deep snow in Belgrade, didn't have shoes, and wanted to get home. They were no different from young sportsmen of today.[19] Thus, it was 3.04 p.m., as the Munich clock on the South East wall of Old Trafford commemorates, when the plane began its last journey. It was to end it ploughing through a fence and then an occupied house (the four people in it were somehow spared), which sent it spinning into a field. The plane broke up in flames. Some didn't get out; a lucky few survived, with the scars they bear to this day.[20]

I was a boy in South East Lancashire at the time and I remember it vividly even now. People often say they remember where they were when Jack Kennedy was assassinated on November 22nd 1963 or when the topless towers of New York City collapsed on September 11th 2001. If I have no particular recollection of my geographical relationship with those events, I have a clear image of myself sitting on the carpet in front of the television screen when the news flashed on about the Munich air crash. I recall, as if it were this day, and I accept that recollection may be faulty with the passage of time, that Cliff Michelmore was compering the 'Tonight' programme and Cy Grant seemed to have penned what is even today sung on the terraces as the 'United Calypso'.[21] Memory can be a perfidious friend but I believe he had just performed it live in honour of the Babes' epic game in Belgrade. Perhaps the news was already in by then and this was part of the vigil, because I seem to recollect that it was a news flash in the middle of the programme which first stunned me into almost incomprehensible awareness. The sense of shock remains with me to this day. I think I spent the night hoping desperately that the news would not be so grim, that it would prove

---

19   For an analysis of Alan Hardaker's (the Football League secretary) position see Jim White *Manchester United: The Biography* (2008)
20   There were 23 fatalities and 21 survivors.
21   Apparently it was first recorded by Edric Connor in 1955. See Davy Collins *A History of the Chants* 2012.

to be exaggerated and this race of supermen would not disappear forever from the annals of football history. At school the next day I was one distraught child among other children from the mill towns of Lancashire who did not care particularly for Manchester United and who made jokes about the news. I may have had more than one fight in the playground that day but, as this was a regular experience for me back in those times, memory might be playing tricks. Perhaps my contemporaries left me alone but I doubt it, knowing the rough humour and *Schadenfreude* of those parts. Coming from one of those mill towns with its own local football tradition, many have asked me why I am a Manchester United fan. I can place it back to even earlier than that bleak February day but, whatever else is said, the memory of that moment is etched fiercely on my heart. It was my first ever brush with mortality and it is one I will never forget. It is a memory similar to that of my grandfather, who took part in one of those epic football matches between the Germans and the British between the lines at Ypres, before going back to making men of dust of men of flesh.[22]

Munich made me a captive to Manchester United. For a football mad kid, and a romantic at heart, no other team would ever do for me. What I have attempted to demonstrate in these pages is how others came to the same realisation. It was easy for my generation, simply because of that monumental tragedy. Those who came later often had to show more fortitude because they did not have that life-defining moment to rely on and there is no doubt that United often tortured even the hardiest soul. What, between us, we have made of the club is something even greater than a mere institution. George Bernard Shaw once said that there is only one religion but there are a hundred versions of it. During the last national census, my fellow fan, the same John Warrington whose question sparked this book, mentioned to me that if every United fan filled in the 'religion' section of his form with "Man United" there would be sufficient adherents for the club to be officially declared a religion.[23] Perhaps

---

22   The recorded instances of this phenomenon are dated at the first Christmas truce (24th December 1914). Reality set in thereafter. It is generally thought the British had the ball and kicked it into No Man's Land but that a German was the emissary of peace.
23   Definitely possible as the Krishna sect has perhaps 1m, Christian Science less than 500,000, Zoroastrianism 200,000. The Jehovah's Witnesses have 6.5m and United (according to BBC

with one eye on the after-life and another on the unfortunate consequences of hubris, not many, as far as I am aware, adopted that course (although I imagine there were some) but the point makes a good deal of sense. You only have to tap into the plethora of messages which flood the ether and the cybernetic highway from home and abroad whenever the Reds play, the highs and lows of mood which follow the team's success or failure, to appreciate the wisdom of Shaw's words. The club is, in a sense, the embodiment of a version of the one religion. Most football teams are to a larger or lesser extent precisely that to their most devoted fans. In United's case, however, the community of the church is broader than any other in the world.

I became, irrevocably, a United fan because of Munich but I was attracted to them first in the 1957 Cup Final. I was from Burnley and in those days the twenty six mile distance between my home town, nestling away in the lee of Pendle Hill, and the big city of Manchester, was a formidable barrier. The bus over the Pennines gave promise of spectacular scenery, however, and was a pleasanter prospect than the ride through the neighbouring towns of Accrington, Blackburn, Darwen and Bolton. The journey was a treat rather than a commonplace so the United matches I was able to take in until much later were few and far between. My mother's anticipation of the age of retail therapy, which manifested itself in a penchant for shopping at Manchester's landmark C&A store, did, however, mean that I got the opportunity more than most from my backwater. The 1957 Cup Final was the first final I ever watched and I did so because my dad, a Burnley supporter back in the days when Burnley had a strong and attractive side, told me that these youngsters were special. They were going to do something unprecedented for many a year and win the double. I remember my sense of childish outrage when Peter McParland got away with little short of murder, reducing the incredibly brave Ray Wood (United's goalkeeper) to a right wing passenger, playing on in an era of no substitutions despite a broken collar bone. McParland scored both Aston Villa goals. I am sure he will have retired ultimately to a

---

News 18th Feb. 2013 based on a Kantar survey of 2012) has 659m fans worldwide. Islam 1.3bn; Christianity 2bn....

profitable career as a pantomime villain. Others felt the same sense of keen disappointment. Wilf McGuinness said, "If we had won the Villa game we would have won the double. I came away from that game in tears. ... That was the first time I saw Duncan Edwards nearly lose his temper. He took three steps forward then stopped and I'm sure he was going to hit him or tell him what he felt ... I was in tears ... because we should have been the first team after the war to win the double ..." [24]

Five of the Busby Babes in happier times.

Wilf was there too (but not a player) for the final of 1958, the year that United wore a shirt with a bird as emblem, which even today is sometimes mistaken for Liverpool's Liver Bird. It was of course the phoenix of the first chapter of this book and it represented the team's recovery from Munich. The game was famous only for yet another charge on a United keeper, when Nat Lofthouse bundled Harry Gregg into the back of the net, Casey and all. Charging the keeper was not then outlawed but Wilf, sitting on the side-lines recovering from a cartilage injury, still felt that goal should not have been allowed.[25] But that's part of the legend of Manchester United: it's

---

24   United We Stand edited by Graham McColl 2002.

not just the stylish victories or the great tragedy; it's the bravery in defeat too.

Duncan Edwards Deceased (1958). The youngest at the time to represent England.

---

25   Ditto.

CHAPTER 3
THE HOLY GRAIL

The European Champions' Cup is the "promised land" of United's aspirations. Yet, only the footballing knights, Busby and Ferguson, have taken the club into this competition. The cup itself was near enough a novelty when Busby took up the chase. His initial interest in it stemmed merely from the natural desire to test the boundaries of his young team. Sadly, because they were not finally to be granted that opportunity which all young athletes desire, to compete in the greatest final against the very best, his interest became an obsession, a means of vindicating the loss of that great side. Winning the European Cup was to be their epitaph, even if only a handful of them could participate in the final victory.

Reading words that the parvenus such as Paddy Crerand have subsequently written brings the understanding that they thought they were not worthy, or this thought was not far from their minds. He looked at the parents and relatives of the fallen, who had been invited to the final, and felt that it was their boys and not him who should have been standing there, savouring this moment.[26]

Ferguson's assault on the greatest of all prizes was driven by another force. He stepped into the legacy of Busby when, arguably, United's powers had seldom been at a lower ebb since the Munich disaster. In truth Busby did not have a worthy successor. It was far too early for someone like Wilf McGuinness to step into that breach. Frank O' Farrell, was competent but his success at Leicester scarcely equipped him for such a high profile job. There were echoes of that after the retirement of Sir Alex with the unfortunate David Moyes. No mean success at Everton, he moved on to prove that a cruiserweight simply does not have the physique to become an effective heavyweight. Tommy Docherty looked and sounded the part and might well have

---

[26] Particularly after meeting Duncan Edwards' mother after the 1968 final. He felt "very humble". See his autobiography: *Never Turn The Other Cheek*.

made the job his own if it had not been for a congenital death wish coupled with a penchant for in-house adultery. Ron Atkinson, too, had a propensity to shoot himself in the foot, or perhaps electrocute himself on the sun bed, whereas his immediate predecessor, Sexton, was a talented coach but might have been too nice to be a manager. It was said that he couldn't hold the dressing room in the early days of player power but perhaps it was again simply a question of the job, the inheritance and the consequent expectation being too big for a mere mortal.

To prove himself worthy of wearing the mantle Sir Alex had to win the First Division (or Premiership as it became in the 1992-3 season) and then the European Cup. If he could do both and do it with a largely home-grown side then he could truly consider himself to have fulfilled the Busby legacy. In so doing, he would add another stirring sentence to the epitaph of the team which perished. The emphasis on the "home-grown" is the one major caveat to that aspiration. Ron Atkinson, for instance, who famously discarded Peter Beardsley because he didn't think he could accommodate him in a team with Mark Hughes (whom he then sold to Barcelona), had no interest in the 'grow-your-own' business. He courted the quick fix, the instant success, the immediate headline. Even if he had not been a serial underachiever, creating teams in the same mould, he was insufficiently "pure" a knight to achieve the Grail. Ferguson would have welcomed the European Cup, however it had come, but in his heart of hearts he knew that the trophy was only truly worth the capture if victory could be achieved with a home-produced side, a reincarnation of the Babes, the once and future team.

The concept of Manchester United FC as yet another thread of Arthurian mythology peculiar to the British people, but adopted throughout the world as the Celtic people's parallel of all tribal 'golden age' myths, will have many readers thinking I'm having a laugh and they would be right in one sense. However, I do think about the club in those romantic terms and not just because Manchester United is about 'fantasy football'. More than any other footballers in the world, even the self-named *galacticos* of Real Madrid, these players are surrounded by a haze of romance. They are the stuff of which myths are made. Despite not having been the most successful team, not only in the world but also in Britain and in England, in the period in which the myth has been woven, United stands supreme as the football team which the world sees as the spirit of romance.

If the club was to become a legend of Arthurian proportions, there was one other ingredient which would add to the myth: the production of legendary players of sublime skill, courage and commitment. This is the other factor which has raised United's profile above those of any other clubs in the minds not only of its own fans but also of the previously uncommitted. It can be argued that Real Madrid's galaxy of superstars outshines United's but that would miss the point. In Real's case the players are virtually all imports. The club is seen as something of a Harlem Globetrotters of the footballing world and it wouldn't really be a great surprise if its publicity machine was suddenly to announce that, from now on, it will only play in exhibition matches. There is something unreal about Real Madrid. There is no romance in sheer fantasy. The fantasy has to reflect real life. You have to be able to believe that it could be you.

In United's case there have been a number of contenders in the post-war era for King of Old Trafford. There are many contenders, but the ones against whom no voice will be raised are, in chronological order: Edwards, Charlton, Law, Best, Robson, Cantona, Giggs, Keane, Beckham, Scholes and Ronaldo. It is interesting perhaps that the line has ended with the magnificent Portuguese number 7. You feel that Rooney, despite phenomenal potential (he was the best youngster I had seen in years when I first saw him at 15 for Everton) has never quite made it and perhaps therein lies the problem of Manchester United in recent years.[27] This category is not about talent and who is the best player but about charisma, which in a number of these exemplars is partially about self-promotion, whereas in others it is not about that at all. It is a category of course which is never closed. Rooney has time yet.

---

27   It is interesting that Paul Scholes thinks Rooney may have peaked at 27. Rooney of course doesn't agree but it was probably true of Best. See BBC Sport 5th June 2014.

The first incarnation of this superman, Duncan Edwards, was a sportsman of whom Bobby Charlton would say that he felt unfit to tie his bootlaces.[28] Edwards was not the captain of the Babes (that honour went to the older Roger Byrne) but he was the acknowledged leader, despite his callowness. A modern player with similar qualities is Liverpool's Stevie Gerrard. Edwards was 21 when he died at Munich. Later that year England would take part in a World Cup which saw the first of Brazil's famous five wins and gave birth to the legend of Pele. How different the team's progress would have been if Edwards and some of his United colleagues (Byrne, Taylor, Pegg for instance) had not died. Indeed, it is more than likely that Big Duncan would still have been around in 1966. What a midfield partner he would have made for Charlton and Moore. Thus, Munich deprived not only United but also the nation as a whole of potential football success.[29]

In the 60's the King mimicked the New Testament and effectively became a Trinity. The continuation of the Edwards line and of the legend was found in Bobby Charlton, then in Denis Law and the Celtic genius, George Best. The Englishman, the Irishman and the Scotsman all had their separate, competing and yet complementary attributes. A reincarnation of this phenomenon occurred in the modern quartet of Beckham, Scholes, Keane and Giggs. However, despite their prowess and before so astonishingly jettisoning David in the direction of the arch-enemy Real Madrid, Ferguson demonstrated, from time to time, that he didn't have absolute faith in that quartet. It was Scholes who has had to change his game to accommodate a new pretender to the King's crown. It is perhaps a pity that Ferguson failed to recognise at the beginning that this quartet was the best in the world. There may or may not have been better players in every position in some other team but nowhere in the world was there a foursome as good, not only for its skill and telepathic ability to read each other's game, but also for its sheer heart and drive.

---

28   Quoted in ONE Love ONE United 1st October 2011.
29   Charlton told the BBC that Duncan's death was the biggest single tragedy to hit English football and his successor Bobby Moore said in his autobiography that there would never be another player like him. The respect for this player is such that it is impossible to believe that he was not as good as they said.

Denis Law in his pomp

Many would say that of the trinity the Irishman was the best by name and by nature but some excellent judges would stand in Bobby Charlton's corner. Pele considered him 'a master footballer'; Beckenbauer considered him 'better even than Pele',[30] whose shirt was pinned to the German's lounge wall. Benfica's manager, Bela Guttman, felt that he was 'the best midfield player in Europe'[31]. His own brother, Jack, in spite of a long standing family rift, told the News of the World in 1973 that "Denis Law may have had more devil, George Best may have been cheekier with the ball, Pele was stronger and had marvellous skills. But I've weighed all this up and I'm convinced that Bobby was the finest all-rounder in the world."[32]

---

30 1975 – quoted in Leo McKinstry's *Jack and Bobby* page 200. In fairness Beckenbauer has made contradictory statements, saying on one occasion that Pele's 20 years at the top marks him as unrivalled by anyone.
31 Ditto. Page 201
32 Ditto.

Bobby is of course a United legend and all he lacks in comparison with the other United legends is the quality he never coveted – charisma, an ability to exploit his own fame. He was the most modest and unassuming of heroes but that does not mean that he wasn't the most talented. He was after all gloriously two-footed and, despite not having been a recognised striker, has a goal ratio of nearly one in two for the national side and nearly one in three for his club. The number of 'assists' he provided for his team-mates must eclipse those figures many times over.

His was and is somehow a very English quality but the world may well have devalued such characteristics in favour of a more flamboyant type of hero. It does not suit the media image of the club's greatest player that he was not a dark Celtic warrior nor had he been brought up on Copacabana beach but he was, instead, an introverted balding man with the most famous "comb-over" in the world. And he hailed from a mining town in Northumberland.

The emergence of George Best and his status as the 'fifth Beatle', the first football celebrity and superstar, is yet another reason why Manchester United rocketed ahead of the opposition of all countries in the popularity stakes. Never had a footballer been the equivalent of a film star or a pop icon before. Best was not only a contributory factor to the Manchester United legend, he was also the reason why it continued to be sustainable even in the drought years. Best was a phenomenon. Many think of him as the best footballer ever. Some put him only behind Pele. Of the top-rated quartet of those years, Pele, Best, Cruyff and Maradona, only the Argentine has enjoyed quite the same high profile and for all the wrong reasons. Not many United fans who have any recall of that era will forget that Best 'retired' from the game (he played for other teams but he had given it up as a serious business) in 1971 at the age of 27. There should have been a great deal left in the locker. Despite his alcoholism he was a prodigious athlete and a competitor of immense courage.

Some see it as George's great betrayal of United, that he deserted the team when it had reached its nadir. There are similarities with press speculation about Wayne Rooney's attitude today, although, even if true, they are differently motivated.

The truth is that the exertions of getting the team back off the ground after the Munich nosedive had probably left it bereft elsewhere and George was probably too much playboy to be hassled with the job of being the club's saviour as well as its talisman. He was no Robson, Keane, or even Cantona.

In mitigation it must be said that standards were slipping across the board. Matters which Busby would have attended to automatically in the pre-Munich era were forgotten in its aftermath. The team had been forced to replace its home grown talent with bought players and, although the conveyor belt had not entirely broken down, its maintenance had become a secondary consideration. The failure of United to win a championship for 26 years after 1967 was, therefore, as much the result of Munich as were any of its frenetic successes in the 60's. The betrayal of Best lies in the perception that, if he had stayed and used his talent responsibly in the 1970's when he was still a young man around whom a fourth great team could have been built, United would not have suffered relegation in 1974 and, accordingly, would not have taken so long to get back to the top. Instead he went off to play for…. Fulham!

The criticism again misses the point. It is of course another of history's what ifs. The betrayal wasn't really a betrayal. The fault lay in the contradictions in George's character. John Challis, the actor who played Boycie of Fools and Horses fame told the story on the television programme *'Loose Women'* (a misnomer if there ever was one) of drinking in a hotel bar until 2 a.m. whilst doing something in the 60's for Granada television. He found himself in the company of a still youthful George Best, wondering how an athlete could drink like that and still play the next day.[33] The sad truth is that, for a very long time, he could and the boy from Belfast had such a phenomenal talent that he was often the best player on the park. The impression abides that if he had looked after himself as Bobby Charlton had, he might well have deserved the accolade of the greatest player ever. No United fan will forget the night in Benfica in the 1966 quarter-

---

33   Loose Women ITV 3rd June 1999

final when Best emerged as the greatest footballer in the world and was nicknamed 'El Beatle'.[34] The Irishman's contribution to the myth of United's once and future king cannot be underestimated. He was the club's greatest player in terms of pure talent and the truth is that he may well have been the world's.

Best and Law hunting in packs (1968)

---

[34]   Estadio da Luz 9th March 1966. The Portuguese media dubbed him *O Quinto Beatle*.

CHAPTER 4
TILTING AT WINDMILLS

After Best it is arguable that United would have to wait a long time for the next coming of the born again United King. Not until another Celt, Eric Cantona, strutted the stage of the Theatre of Dreams would men talk around the hearth in the terms of the heroes of old, the men of genius, the gods. This of course ignores inspirational England captain, Bryan Robson. Chester-le-Street born Robbo was unlucky to play for United in their largely under-achieving period when Liverpool ruled the roost but, not only for his sheer ability but also for his inspirational qualities, he deserves to be counted among that elite group of special players who have created the 'Romance' of United. If he had any weakness, it lay in the fact that he was too good, too inspirational. The team became a one man team and there was always the impression that if anyone was going to pull something out of the fire it would be Skip. One reason Paul Gascoigne gave for not choosing United before Spurs was that he feared Robson would be too protective. Robson had to move over before Ince could come through and Ince had to go to make room for Keane.

In the interim a number of gifted players have graced the playing fields of Manchester United. The most celebrated and one whose gifts are underestimated by some had to leave for the same Real Madrid we have considered at length in these pages. I don't think for one moment he wanted to leave and United's preferred destination of choice for him was Barcelona but once they decided he was expendable, he chose his own destiny.[35] David Beckham's obvious counterweight in the United side was Ryan Giggs. The Welshman with the broad Lancashire accent was gifted in those mercurial ways which are so different from the Essex boy's. Beckham was however in the earlier years more beloved on the Old Trafford terraces because - again, it is a working class thing - there was greater

---

35   Daniel Taylor The Guardian and Gabriele Marcotti on CNNSI.com 12th June 2003.

appreciation of his graft, just as there was with Keane and Scholes. Giggs has been known to shy away from a tackle; he is a great header of the ball but he doesn't much like his head being used as a conker. I have never quite understood the mentality of those who believed that the Welshman, with all his subtlety, should be forcing himself into leg-breaking tackles. He always did his share of supporting the back players and I found utterly inane the criticism of the terrace know-alls, for whom the penny had not dropped, that he did not put his life sufficiently on the line. In the mid 2000's they still yelled at Giggs to take up station on the left wing, assuming it was some errant flaw in his character, rather than the instructions of his manager, which led him to drift inside.[36]

Beckham's right foot is a little short of a gift from God and Giggs' ability to dribble at speed, his capacity for running with the ball at the very edge of control, is as divine as it gets in sports terms. It lifts the crowd, gets even his detractors out of their seats. Giggs has suffered in comparison with Best but that is again the result of a flaw in the perspective. Bryan Robson was compared with Duncan Edwards, as was Roy Keane. The comparisons simply don't work. Giggs has more in common with Bobby Charlton in his self-effacement and that may also be one reason why he had his detractors on the terraces. He was not interested in the kind of charisma which Cantona, Best and Beckham coveted. Any charisma he owns is derived from his ability on the ball. It is probably fair to say that the good-goody two shoes images was severely dented by John Hemming MP's revelation under the dubious protection of parliamentary privilege that the apparently shy and certainly self-effacing Giggs had obtained a super-injunction to cover up an adulterous affair, although it is fair to say also that the onset of social media had by this time made the revelation academic.[37] It might also be added that the tarnishing of the image did him no harm on those same terraces, no matter what "right-thinking" people elsewhere may have thought of it, but it made for some entertaining songs from rival supporters. Giggs simply played through them, but the storm

---

36   Giggsy's record now speaks for itself, playing with dignity and no diminution of ability (as opposed to stamina) until he was 40 and then taking the helm as interim manager after David Moyes was dismissed.

37   BBC News 23rd May 2011.

broke immediately before United's renewal of hostilities with Barcelona in yet another Champions League final in May 2011. From that point of view, the one which would most bother him, the timing was scarcely helpful. The question of whether the adverse publicity actually got in the way of a knighthood is more conjectural.[38]

David Beckham would, of course, have been the choice of many (before his departure for Real Madrid) for the owner of that tag as the descendant of the Magi of the United game. He deserves the accolade for many reasons but it is a trophy which can only be awarded in a team setting. A player is only as good or as god-like as his team-mates permit him to be. The history of the game is replete with fantastic players who played with men whose god-like footballing feet were actually made of clay. In that context few would argue with the point that the player Manchester United miss most of all from their "class of 1992" is Paul Scholes. The Oldham man's silky all round skills and vision mark him out as one of the world's great midfielders, an opinion subscribed to by no lesser luminaries than Zinedine Zidane[39] and Xavi Hernandez[40] both the greatest midfield players of their generation.

Players become legends for many different reasons. Ole Gunnar Solskjaer, for instance, is just accepted by Reds' fans as a 'Red'. It is a given that he will die for the cause. Ruud Van Nistelrooy on the other hand is a legend simply because of what he achieved in United colours, even though his stay at the club bisected two of its most productive European eras. Then of course there is Cristiano Ronaldo who is still re-writing records at Real Madrid but transformed himself at United from talented show pony to arguably the greatest footballer in the world, an accolade he has exchanged on occasions with his great contemporary, Lionel Messi of Barcelona.

All these remarks lead ultimately to the comment that it is unfair in the context of a team game to single out individuals but of course a club must have its heroes. They are essential to keep the crowds

---

38   See e.g The Guardian 30th September 2010
39   Daily Mirror 22nd August 2010 in a direct interview.
40   Telegraph 31st May 2011.

coming in. The judgment of the present is biased. George Best, ever an egomaniac, never accepted during his lifetime his relegation to second spot in the pantheon of United greats behind Cantona, but it is inevitable, given that many more of those who voted have seen Cantona. Only a limited few will have seen Best and, it has to be said, many of those will have voted in the belief that the past is always better than the present. It is the tragedy of all performing arts that the career is always a brief candle. The ever-increasing media record helps to preserve the record but so often it simply looks out of date and context.

Cantona himself probably gave Best the greatest compliment ever when he said at the time of the Irishman's funeral, "after his first training session in heaven George Best from the favourite right wing turned the head of God who was filling in at left back.... I would love him to save me a place in his team, George Best that is, not God."[41] I am not surprised that George, ever the egotist, was unhappy at being placed behind Cantona, even though, in footballing terms, there were at least three generations between them, but he would probably be even less so at Giggs having been voted the club's best player ever, which really demonstrates that these things are very much of their time.[42]

The truth is that the past and the present are different countries and there is no point in comparing anything more than records. In terms of records the present generation of players long ago surpassed their 1960's predecessors, although again we run into difficulties when we seek to make any comparison with the Babes. The class of 92 suffers from the same defect which the 60's side had and which did not seem to be inherent in the makeup of the Babes. They didn't actually believe they were the best, not at least globally. Perhaps those early defeats by a Barca managed by Johann Cruyff and led by Koeman

---

41   Patrick Reilly Goal Magazine 28th October 2010 (but the comment was made in 2005)
42   Cantona - Inside United Magazine 2001 and Giggs - Official Man United Website 31st January 2011. On balance for those who have seen all three can one really argue that Best was anything other than the greatest player of his all too brief time and equally so of United's history?

Eric Cantona - Le Roi Nouveau

and Stoichkov took their toll in leaving a seed of doubt. The 60's side could produce the fantastic 5-1 victory in Lisbon and then go out in the semis to the journeymen of Partizan Belgrade. They could win the European Cup in style (at least in extra time) in 1968 but give way too easily to a spiteful Estudiantes in the World Club Championship. The abiding impression was that the guys whom Busby had to buy in to replace the Babes forever lost in the woods of time did not really want it quite so badly. They liked the adventure but winning wasn't always everything. They could look themselves in the mirror when they lost. The current crop seemed to have overcome that particular chimera in 1999 at the Nou Camp but it resurfaced, with that same complacency which the 60's side would from time to time show, when they were asked to repeat the feat, not only in 2000 but also in 2001, 2002 and 2003. In the latter year the team finally found its feet and at last outplayed Real Madrid at Old Trafford only to discover that the cavalry charge was, like the famous one at Balaclava, too light and too late.

This was more evidence of slipping back into the bad old ways. The underachievement of "the kids" in Europe (prior to 1999 and "after the promised land") is a symptom of a phenomenon which I described earlier. You should not go into a "negotiation" without a sense of your own superiority. United's youngsters found themselves in a situation in which a few more experienced big-timers would have been a benefit. They were unlucky in that they caught the end of the era in which UEFA could dictate, in opposition to European legal rules about freedom of movement etc., that teams could field only a limited number of foreign (or even assimilated) players. Not even Eric had the experience to counterbalance the weakening of a side which could not field Giggs and Hughes (because they were Welsh), Irwin and Keane (because they were Irish) as well as Kanchelskis and Schmeichel.

Indeed, the mauling the depleted team received at the hands of top opposition like Johann Cruyff's Barcelona in their formative years may well have instilled an element of self-doubt into these young and impressionable minds, one which was difficult subsequently to overcome. Like glandular fever it was always waiting to return so that even after the exorcism of the Nou Camp 1999 it appeared only too willing to reassert itself the next season. A complacent United ran into another underachieving side in Real Madrid in the quarter finals of the European Cup. They then went out at the same stage to Bayern Munich in 2001 and to the relatively mediocre opposition of Leverkusen in 2002 before a total loss of confidence in Madrid, regained splendidly but insufficiently in the return at Old Trafford in 2003, cost them potential success in a final on their own ground. Any football fan who witnessed the turgid affair served up by Juventus and A.C. Milan must have quaked in their boots at the thought that this could be the future. Only Liverpool fans would have cheered, believing that there can be a second coming. "What rough beast, its hour come round at last, slouches towards Anfield to be born?"[43]

The 1999 European Cup win was a brilliant achievement, victory snatched from the jaws of defeat, but it was also fortuitous, a typical Manchester United *tour de force*. Roy Keane was the first to

---

[43] With apologies to W.B. Yeats - The Second Coming.

Cole and Yorke with the Grail (1999)

appreciate this. His vocalisation of these doubts cannot have endeared him to many of his team-mates but they were true. Other teams with fewer resources have demonstrated even in the 90's that achievements can be serial. Something had to be done. The something was of course that Ferguson got on to his fourth team, or was it his fifth?

The difficulty he then faced was that his teams had only recently learned how to be better than the Italians and the Germans but the Spaniards, in particular Real Madrid, refused to stand still at the same time. He was still playing catch up and for all Manchester United's financial success as probably the only truly profitable of the big clubs, the only one which had not enjoyed some sort of subsidy from wealthy individuals or corporations, he was not able to compete in the money-no-object market. He had deep pockets but not the deepest.

This has always been the case in Europe, even if the main opponent has changed from time to time. Now it does not even hold good in England and even Ferguson faced the unpalatable fact that, in a head to head challenge with Chelsea and Manchester City for the same player, he would only succeed in the unlikely modern scenario that the matter did not come down solely to money. His reaction to the Russian revolution was spectacular and emphatic and the signs were that he would deal with the Arab billions in the same way. I wrote back in 2006 that if he succeeded, despite those odds, his United epitaph would truly give him the credit of finally eclipsing even Sir Matt but if he failed then his reputation would not be so much tarnished as incomplete. I have to say that he did not fail but that is not the whole of the or even half of his story.

CHAPTER 5
THE RELIGION

That the club is legendary (in the sense that its fans forever look back on a golden age to draw their parallels with their contemporaries) is not unusual. All teams have their special years and, more often than not, it is the fans who span more than one generation who can be found looking nostalgically back over their shoulders in a continual comparison of players of today and their counterparts of yesteryear. In United's case, however, it is something more than mere nostalgia. Fans who have never been to Old Trafford, including some too young to remember Bryan Robson with any clarity, let alone the Babes or Best, Law and Charlton, have tapped into the spiritual soul of the club. United has become the once and future team. Its greatest players, a continuous vein of whom can be traced from the post-war years to the millennium, are the embodiment of the perfect warrior. One might as well believe that he will return at the end of the time and redeem all things. In this way United has an advantage over its rivals because, at various times in the club's history, it has been able to field the embodiment of the once and future king - whether in the guise of the original Scotsman to hold the title, the perfect French chevalier who would illuminate the field of dreams in the 90's, or the Iberian talisman who would be his successor. If all these men could play together then surely United would have the celestial team. All fans of all clubs are able to choose their ideal eleven from the archives, but is it just me or does there really remain the sneaking feeling that only one team will get to play in heaven?

The question of the birth and re-birth of the United hero and his status as King of Old Trafford has demonstrated that he can be either home-grown or imported. History dictates that many have been imported, even though the purist would prefer the champion to be one of his own. The most famous of the imports is of course Eric Cantona, whom many believe to have been home-grown in any event. Certainly he 'came home' to Old Trafford when he joined in

1992 and, if his talent was mercurial before, it flowered in the red and white. Similar thoughts must have applied to Denis Law when he also came to his spiritual home precisely thirty years earlier for a then record transfer fee of £115,000. United fans prefer to forget that he played twice for City and that he was the discovery of Bill Shankly when he was manager of Huddersfield Town. It doesn't matter therefore that the son was prodigal.

The peculiar attraction of the Babes and then of George Best was that they were entirely home-grown. In the Babes' case it seemed that a team made largely in Manchester might be the best in the world. The chances of that happening ever again in a century, let alone a generation, were scarce. It certainly did happen with Glasgow Celtic's 'Lisbon Lions' but it was a comparative rarity. Ajax demonstrated the ability to rise to the top time and time again with a largely Dutch side and Bayern Munich continue to recreate themselves with a majority of German players, although the stars are often foreigners. The great AC Milan side always had a hard core of Italian players to support the 'flair' foreigners. Real Madrid perhaps has fewer native born Spanish players in its current manifestation than would have been expected a generation ago but there is still a strong nucleus of Spaniards and there is a feeling that these form a clique at the club and rumours of this resurface from time to time.

A special position is always reserved in the heart of any club's supporters for the product of their youth teams but, equally often, those same supporters have to look far afield for their super-heroes. Not many in the present day would doubt for instance that Manchester United's celestial team, the one which will play at the end of the world against all the forces of darkness, will be captained by a Frenchman who made the high collar his trade mark. There are many other contenders for the role but could any acquit themselves quite so well as the Gallic genius, Cantona?

Best with the Ballon d'Or (1968)

Many football fans worship their club. Manchester United is not special in that regard. Not many clubs have the kind of following of Manchester United. It is one of the perpetual sneers that United fans generally come from anywhere other than Manchester. The nouveau-riche Manchester City famously started a propaganda movement in the city to proclaim itself *Real* Manchester, playing on the idea that all true Mancunians support the Blues and importing the rather contrary notion that it is somehow akin to the fabulous Madrid club, which of course vies with United for the global following. The idea is of course nonsense. No club will survive in its own back yard without a matrix of indigenous fans and City's bogus claim is little more than an attempt to give an impression with words which it has failed in the past to achieve with deeds. What is difficult to understand is how a football club from a city on the north of England, not even in political terms the second let alone the first city, has achieved a status of which all clubs, with the possible rare exceptions of Real Madrid and, latterly, Barcelona, are envious.

Why? Why is it that United, rather than, for instance, the phenomenally successful Liverpool of the 70's and 80's, or Real Madrid, the team named by FIFA as the greatest club ever, stood at the pinnacle of the game in the early part of this millennium and still has the largest world-wide following? Why is it even up there? Why is this team from industrial Lancashire the team of choice to a crushing majority of football supporters all over the world? The reason is of course shrouded in history. History alone, however, is too one-dimensional to make heroes of mortals. Thus, there is a point in the story of Manchester United where history plays truant. It slips surreptitiously out of the back door into the country known as legend. This is of course as much reminiscent of the Christian myth as the Arthurian, the latter of which may in any event derive at least in part from the former.

United was not one of the founder members of the Football League. All of the clubs who enjoyed that distinction are still around today but their fortunes have fluctuated with the football seasons.[44] United was founded by the railway workers of the Lancashire and North East Railway (LNER) Newton Heath in 1874[45] and although the club's early history was one of relatively smooth progress it could scarcely be described as an unmitigated success. Indeed, the first 50 years were fairly run of the mill. United enjoyed their championship successes and their FA Cup triumphs in their early years but it cannot be said that in the period before the second world war they were the pre-eminent team in England, or, indeed, in Manchester itself, where their rivals, Manchester City, had an equal if not slightly better record.

If you believe the 'Blue' propaganda, City are the true Manchester Club, but in fact the City was formed, later than United, from West Gorton St. Marks in 1881, re-named as Ardwick FC in 1887. They did however adopt the sobriquet of Manchester City in 1894, eight years before the 'Heathens' rejected Manchester Central and Manchester Celtic (a name considered no doubt in honour of the club's vast Irish immigrant following in the city even at that time) and the team became known by the name it bears today.

It is possibly of some significance that the two Manchester teams

---

44   Accrington F.C (not Accrington Stanley, which was a later-formed local rival), Aston Villa, Blackburn Rovers, Bolton Wanderers Burnley, Derby County, Everton, Notts County, Preston North End, Stoke City, West Bromwich Albion, Wolverhampton Wanderers.

45   Newton Heath in eastern Manchester was the western end of the line just as Leeds was the eastern.

came into existence in the same era as the Manchester Ship Canal, the emblem of which both clubs bear on their arms to this day. It is significant because the Ship Canal, which has of course declined as the waterway of industry since the Second World War, was the true mark of the arrival of Manchester as England's citadel of the north.[46] Manchester started life as part of the old Saxon Salford Hundred. Its population in 1801 was 322,000. By 1850 it was over one million and by 1901 it had doubled again. The population explosion was the result of the cotton industry but Manchester was simultaneously developing leading edge technology in the manufacture of machinery for textile production and its new found confidence had discovered one major hurdle to success. Yes, you've guessed it: Liverpool! The Merseyside city's harbour dues were prohibitive for Manchester goods. They were deemed so extortionate by Mancunian businessmen that Oldham merchants of the period found it cheaper to transfer goods 100 miles to Hull and ship them from there rather than deliver them the 30 miles to Liverpool and suffer the reduction of profitability from Scouse profiteering.[47]

There must be many explanations nowadays for the vitriolic outpourings which rain down from the terraces every time Scousers and Mancs join battle on the football field. However, the rivalry between these two neighbouring northern cities actually stems from that time when the new town of Manchester believed its hard-working population to have suffered exploitation from Liverpool wharfies, who were perceived as sitting on their backsides, collecting their unearned dues from the hard-working but landlocked neighbour along the East Lancs Road. It is of course a tribal thing rather than one rooted in fact but Liverpool folk have suffered ever since from the unjust accusation of idleness.[48]

The Manchester Ship Canal Company was formed in 1882 and

---

[46] If Manchester had been adopted as the capital of the Union between Scotland and England there would probably not now be the same evidence of the southern bias which has plagued the relationship since its inception in 1603.

[47] David Owen's *The Manchester Ship Canal* (1983) published by Manchester University Press.

[48] Summed up for some by the brilliant 1982 Alan Bleasdale drama of *Boys from the Blackstuff*, although the continual refrain of one of its main characters, Yosser Hughes (portrayed magnificently by Bernard Hill), was *"gizza job"* and *"I can do that"* (said of rivals in work).

construction began in 1887. It opened in 1894. Manchester City showed commendable opportunism in one of the few occasions when they would be ahead of United by cashing in with their name change. The upshot of the Canal, however, was that Liverpool entered into terminal decline as the business went upriver. You can hear today on the terraces of Anfield and Old Trafford the bitter echoes of the resentment of those times. The feud is not all about whose football team is the more successful, although very few of the people who abuse each other so foully from the home and away ends, will appreciate or care about the genesis of their apparent hatred for each other.

The early days of the two Manchester teams were not markedly different, City perhaps having the edge before the war. City, however, also had one other advantage over United in the immediate post-war period. They had a stadium. German bombers had reduced Old Trafford to rubble, thereby achieving what, 58 years later, Lothar Matthaus and his Bayern Munich team found impossible. United had to ground-share with City, something which, despite the apparent advance of civilisation in other respects, is near inconceivable today. And, despite City's change in fortunes, it remains more than merely doubtful that it could fill Old Trafford.

CHAPTER 6
THE HOME FRONT

So the earliest form of the second and greater question posed (which is derived from the one posed by John Warrington at the beginning of this book) should be, why, out of these two ordinary clubs, Manchester United, finished football's first full century as undisputed champions of Europe (to which the World Club Championship was later added), whilst their nearest rivals, with many advantages over the 'Reds', were battling to achieve promotion from the Nationwide Second Division? The clubs' respective achievements of the treble year are ironically similar to those of 1968 when City won their only Championship before the millennium but United won the European Cup. The Reds upstaging the Blues has a familiar ring.

It would be easy to put the failure down to City complacency. The Blues' former reputation as a yo-yo club scarcely does justice to an abundance of natural resources. However, the fact that, at the turn of the millennium and beyond (and but for a happy accident), United had not only eclipsed its nearest neighbours, but had equally left every single one of its would be rivals languishing in its wake, not only in England but in the world, takes the matter out of the merely parochial. In the hotbed of association football, which has been and is industrial Lancashire, the Reds have disappeared out of sight in terms of popularity and world-wide prestige in comparison with all the old greats like Preston North End, Bolton Wanderers, Blackburn Rovers, Burnley and Everton. All of those clubs were founder members of the Football League.

More particularly, they have totally outstripped Liverpool FC, despite the Merseysiders being the darlings of a media whose gurus were football spectators (probably, in most cases, of the armchair kind) in the days when Kevin Keegan and (after him) Kenny Dalglish and their respective team-mates ruled the roost. Liverpool may have had their seasons in the sun but, for all the club's historic achievements, it is not as famous as Manchester United. Neither is it as universally loved nor, conversely, and this may be more important, as universally loathed.

The suggestion that Manchester United is a more famous club than Liverpool is a bone of contention on Merseyside where the red half of that City once pointed to the fact that United had not won as many league titles. That came to an end in 2009 and now United, with twenty titles, is two in front.[49]

If success in Europe is to be seen as the crowning achievement, Liverpool has had five triumphs in the Champions' Cup to United's three and two in the UEFA cup to United's nil. Having said that, Liverpool's second triumph in the UEFA (in 2001) was in a weakened competition, more akin to United's win in the Cup Winner's Cup (1991) than the old UEFA Cup. Indeed, the point may well be made that most of Liverpool's European triumphs were won when the European game was in financial meltdown and Italian and Spanish teams in particular were severely depleted of their normal quota of foreign players as a result. What a shame! That would be unfair and would detract from Liverpool's immense achievements.

The accusation, however, that Liverpool achieved its successes by a triumph of utilitarian team-work over style is more pervasive. The club has tended to produce functional teams and, even though Kevin Keegan and Kenny Dalgish may be lauded on Merseyside as the greatest footballers ever, no one would put them in the same league as some of United's great players. Liverpool is simply not a team of Romance.

Bone of contention or not, it is most certainly history now and, if Liverpool has had that greater recent record, before the advent of the Premier League in 1993, the question has to be asked, why has the club not taken better advantage of it? Liverpool has not recovered from that black day at Heysel in Brussels on 29th May 1985 when the

---

49   There was some hope on Merseyside and in the media that Liverpool's long count would come to an end in 2014 but, of course, in a year of real nadir for United, City triumphed. It is hard to choose between the worst of two evils but the United / Liverpool divide is still so great that most United supporters prefer the City success.

Merseyside supporters ran amok and caused the deaths of thirty-nine unfortunate supporters of the Italian giant, Juventus.[50] The team may still be able to more or less match Manchester United, from time to time, on the playing field. Most clubs tend to raise their game for the occasion of a visit to or from United. That is even more the case when local rivalries are involved, whereas United quite often play well within their capabilities. Over the past few seasons Liverpool has enjoyed some decent days against the Manchester Reds. However, the gap in superiority overall is such that it has been clear, over recent times, that the fixture means more to the Merseysiders than it does to United which, traditionally, seems to have bigger fish to fry.

It is, therefore, a simple truism that, for one reason or another, Liverpool teams, for all their recent, great past, are now just another small vessel plying in the wake of the great red and white cruiser as she makes progress at a rate of knots over a distant horizon. It is as if all the other clubs have simply lain at anchor, captivated by the vision of this most majestic of liners as she clears the harbour walls and "gropes like a mad world westward".[51] They are like the spectators on the bankside who watch the passage of the QE2.

This is true of overseas rivals as well as United's domestic opponents. Even Real Madrid, the most successful team of all time in terms of results on the pitch, only belatedly woke up to United's disappearing trick and has had to play catch-up, although no one can deny that it has done so successfully, and this is indeed one of the fundamental points of this book. Despite the laudatory account of the Madridistas by John Carlin, whose propositions are essentially theoretical as they are tested over too short a time, the fact is that Real Madrid has had to emulate United rather than United trying to emulate Madrid.[52] The results have yet to be analysed but, although there may be some short-term shift of emphasis, the long term

---

50   14 Liverpool fans were found guilty of manslaughter. The 3 years sentences were seen in Turin at least as derisory and the relationship with Juve has never been repaired. The club suffered another tragedy at Hillsborough on 15th April 1989 when 96 people died and a further 766 were injured. The controversy of the original inquest findings rumble on to this day and the EWHC has in 2014 ordered a new inquest some 25 years after the event.
51   From *Seventy Feet Down* by Philip Larkin.
52   *White Angels* Bloomsbury 2004

position is unlikely to change fundamentally for reasons which will become clear.

Recently we have another new development: the emergence of super-rich individuals who fancy raising their social profiles by getting a piece of the football action. The trend didn't exactly begin with Roman Abramovich, the new owner of the previously. Perennially underachieving Chelsea FC, but he certainly epitomises the new breed and, before the emergence of Manchester City's Abu Dhabi owner, Sheikh Mansour, the Russian was by far the wealthiest of them. He showed himself initially as the most benevolent of dictators but soon proved adept with the long knives as he went through ten managers in five years. Only time will tell if the latest incumbent proves more successful in avoiding the culling.[53]

The history of Abramovich is, however, shrouded in secrecy. One of the oligarchs who benefitted when, in the mid 1990's, the Yeltsin government sold off the oil and gas assets of the allegedly newly-emancipated Russian nation to a group of insiders, he became party to what must rank as one of the most corrupt betrayals of a people throughout the annals of modern history. Downtrodden for centuries by the Czars, living in near Dark Age conditions compared to the West, the Russians saw the ray of hope represented by communism shattered into a million fragments by the excesses of Lenin, Stalin, Brezhnev and a succession of others. They are a tortured people and when, in the late 80's and early 90's of the twentieth century, the Communist stranglehold on Eastern Europe was finally weakened, the wealth which was available to build a new economic miracle went to the very few, who simply preyed like cannibals on their brothers and sisters.

The fate of millions of his own countrymen was perhaps nothing to Abramovich and his type who may, for all I know, be a clutch of sociopaths with a pervasive disregard of the rights of others. His personal interest did not appear initially to be in football but Chelsea was a fashionable enough club for him to see it as the means to bankroll a grand entrance into London High Society and perhaps

---

53   At the time of writing the gracious and dignified Manuel Pellegrini.

provide him with some protection from the new czars at home.[54] Abramovich's arrival in London came very shortly after the arrest and imprisonment (following a show trial reminiscent of the regimes of Stalin and Brezhnev) of another oligarch, Mikhail Khodorkovsky (who was in 2004 reputed to be the sixteenth richest man on the planet), on allegations of fraud. No one, not even Roman Abramovich, was entirely safe from the Putin regime.[55] Even so, Jack Walker proved with Blackburn Rovers, who were Premiership champions in 1995 but now are currently mired in the Championship, that it is possible to buy short term success. No one turned that into relentless success before Abramovich, even allowing for his ruthless disposal of managers who did not deliver the kind of success which he craved, until he was forced to climb down from his first dismissal and reappoint the perennial achiever, Jose Mourinho, in 2013.[56]

So this now begs another question, one which is, however, a variation on the same theme. Just how has Manchester United stolen a march on some of worldwide football's sharpest operators? It is not as if the club was possessed of financial gurus with greater acumen and savvy than all these other clubs. Far from it: United's previously most successful chairman, Martin Edwards, had so much economic perspicuity that he tried, famously, to flog the club to a schoolmaster with absolutely no football credentials other than an ability to do keepie-ups in front of a capacity Old Trafford crowd. Even when he found out that the would-be purchaser was a charlatan, Edwards showed all the financial shrewdness of a butcher's boy as he rewarded Michael Knighton's failure to raise the promised cash by the extended deadline with a seat on the Manchester United Board! One can only assume that he felt Michael

---

54   In reality there is only one Czar, the unprepossessing but apparently fascinating Vladimir Putin, who is now rumoured to have arrogated to himself a wealth which may very well in due course rival that of the Abu Dhabi royal family.

55   See e.g BBC News 31st May 2005.

56   There has been a lot of conjecture about whether the Portuguese was in line for the Old Trafford job. He seemed to have a good relationship with Ferguson but it may have been of the *Godfather* type of keeping friends close and enemies closer. It is hard to see how his abrasive and confrontational style would have worked with the Glazer ownership but he was certainly one of the few up to the job and the rumours of his disappointment that it was given instead to a non-achiever are certainly credible.

might be helpful in club transfer negotiations in view of his ability to pull the wool over everyone's eyes. If Edwards had egg on his face, however, it can have been nothing compared to how Michael Knighton must feel now when he looks at the price for which the club was sold to the Glazers. Failure to get hold of that sum must haunt his dreams of avarice to this day.[57]

Of course the reality now is the west wind from America. Michael Knighton, Martin Edwards and even Rupert Murdoch pale into insignificance against the arrival of the Glazers and the effective use of the company's assets to fund their acquisition.[58] It is an extraordinary fact that a football club of the stature of Manchester United has fallen into the hands of a wealthy family from a country, which has no real feel for the British national game.

However, the seeds of what some see as destruction were sown in the flotation of the club on the Stock Market. Prior to that it was cloth caps on the terraces against starched shirts in the directors' box. Now it is more Gap and Tommy Hilfiger, Daks and Giorgio Armani. In St. Paul's parlance everyone needs a prick to kick against and it is common knowledge that United's Board (of whatever generation) is about as competent and is as well-liked by the fans as the average Highways Agency road-repairing crew is by motorists confronted with miles of red cones and not a workman in sight.[59] So nothing much has changed there. Now it is a family of Yanks who haven't got a clue about running a football club, or so the received wisdom goes. No one can figure out why they wanted it so badly, or how it fell into their hands with so little struggle. Did someone

---

57   His resignation from the board in 1992 to acquire Carlisle United really says it all. But people forget two side issues about this: the first is that his famous ball-juggling act at the opening match against Arsenal of the 1989-90 season took the spotlight away from Neil Webb whose debut it was and who marked it with a brilliant volleyed goal. The second is that Knighton wasn't Martin Edwards' first choice of exit route. He'd tried to sell out to Robert Maxwell five years earlier and how might that have turned out?

58   This was actually supposed to be against the law because the acquisition depended ultimately on leveraging United's assets. The fact that the leveraging occurred *ex post facto* should not have been allowed to disguise the fact that the deal depended on the fact that the underlying transaction was a breach of the Companies Act whitewash rules. This is the old argument that the law is too lax if it allows loopholes to overcome fundamental principles. I suspect that today this transaction would be challenged.

59   There is an echo of this sentiment in Roy Keane's "prawn sandwiches" comment after the Dynamo Kiev match in 2000.

expect the government to intervene to protect what it has described as the crown jewels of English football heritage? If so, they were quickly disappointed, the F.A expressing itself satisfied with the Glazers' plans for the future of the club.

Shareholders United has its quota of financially astute personnel. Their continued certainty that the Glazers simply cannot extract enough cash from the business to bankroll plans, which even the United Chief Executive, David Gill, described as aggressive before he made his U turn and decided to stay on board the apparently sinking ship, is unnerving to those who want to see Manchester United successful no matter who is in charge. And it was a touch risible for those who have not made anything like the Glazers to assert that the recently deceased Malcolm and his sons must have lost their marbles. The simple fact is, here is a family which has made a fortune out of a sports franchise in a respectable, regulated economy. Is it likely that they would have spent so much to buy Manchester United without a plan? That would be extremely careless of individuals who are not famed for their lack of preparation and whose takeover campaign was so clearly straight out of the *Blitzkrieg* textbook that it might have been devised by Erwin Rommel. Make no mistake: the family may have borrowed heavily and from the hedge funds too but they had certainly put at risk at least half of their own wealth if this enterprise had gone down the pan. Thus, the notion should not be dismissed so quickly that they had prepared properly for the circumstances in which they found the club.

The plan was, as it now turns out from at least a partially successful execution, founded on the initial belief, based on their experience of their American football franchise in Tampa, Florida, that, contrary to the ill-informed assertions of journalists and other pundits, United could make more money from television globally. They may regret the fact that they made their move so late. Is it likely that, if they had then been the owners, they would have let David Beckham leave for such modest returns? They expressed themselves always as being fully behind Sir Alex but are they likely to look at that piece of business as good for the Glazer United? It looked at the time as if Sir Alex was attempting to wrest control of the dressing room back from the perceived threat of the Beckham road-show but is it actually a case that no one player is bigger than Manchester United, although the manager might perceive himself as just that? After all it wasn't his first error of judgment.

The wounded Beckham after "Bootgate" (2003)

No one on the terraces really understands to this day the Jaap Stam sale. The Dutchman didn't enjoy the best of seasons after his 1999 triumph and his Achilles tendon injury may well have slowed him down but his success in the Italian Serie A demonstrates that there was plenty yet in the big man's locker. Was that a fit of Ferguson pique? The betting is that the sale of Beckham certainly was. Then there was the Rock of Gibraltar. The damaging dispute over this famous racehorse's stud rights is blamed by many fans for the decision by the Irish millionaires to sell their shares to the Glazer family. This is, however, unrealistic. John Magnier and J. P. McManus had no choice other than to sell. If they hadn't the value of their shares would have plummeted more quickly than a sky-diver whose chute has failed to open. The more interesting point is that, equally, the Glazers had to buy. If they had given into the fan pressure and sold it would have been a fire sale and an admission that the constitution of United had in fact, unwittingly, landed a golden share in the laps of the supporters. In other words, there would have been no buyers at the hiked up price which followed in the wake of the Irish stake-building. The Glazers went for broke and, in doing so, revealed the kind of courage, which makes nonsense of the crude taunts of the anti-takeover lobby.

The reasons for the Glazers' takeover will be debated more fully elsewhere in this book but to deal with the other question of why they were able to steamroller the opposition is distinctly easier. The opposition was in fact always fragmented and simply wasn't ready for the speed of the Glazer assault. The Maginot line was always the Irish duo and their satellites. Conflicting reports came out of this fortress from the very beginning. Dermot Desmond[60], a man close to the Irish tycoons, seemed reassuring. They wouldn't sell. This was, however, a game of bluff, counter-bluff and doublespeak. It was quite pathetic to see the same United faithful, which had lambasted John Magnier mercilessly from the terraces at the height of the *Rock of Gibraltar* dispute, suddenly huddled together in their pubs somehow believing that this maligned millionaire might prove to be their salvation.

Unlike the Germans in World War 11, the Glazers didn't try to outflank this particular fortress. They just stuck to their guns, wouldn't increase their offer over £3 per share, and finally the towering walls crumbled. After that it was a game of dominoes. Shareholders United were beaten before they started. In truth the seeds of their own destruction had been sown much earlier in their complacency after the abortive Murdoch attempt at a takeover of

---

60   The Irish majority shareholder in Celtic FC has always been closer to the Glasgow club than to United and sold out speedily to the Glazers in 2005 for a tidy profit.

United.[61] Their failure to appreciate the strategic importance of the Irish holding was fatal and it may be that, if they had been able to counter-offer a medium term buy out of these shares, it would have fallen on receptive ears. One can't help but be left with the impression that the decision of some of this group now to refuse to attend the club's matches is not only sour grapes but also a decision which would have been made anyway because the gravy train had come to an end. Some at least of them are glory-hunters and it would not be surprising to see the London banker and professional contingent wash up now at Chelsea. Their refusal to deal in any way with the Glazer family and to fight a war of attrition were mistakes as fatal in their way as their failure to have any plan B.

The second thing which the Glazers probably saw long in advance of any of their detractors was that, if the thorny problem of the inherited debt could be safely negotiated, it was not difficult to contemplate a Manchester United which was far more successful in private hands than it was as a Plc. The impression is that the flotation gave United a kick-start in the early nineties but that it had very much had its day, particularly with the emergence of Abramovich and his sleeker, less transparent financial model, by the mid-noughties of the new millennium. The truth is that United's apparent world-wide financial hegemony was never translated into transfer success. There were spectacular pay-outs for Veron, Rio and Wayne Rooney, but the overall suspicion was that if United found itself in a straight fight with Real Madrid, Florentino Perez would win. United's Stock Market restrictions would conspire against them, telegraphing to all their rivals precisely where they intended to strike next. It is like a cobra requesting its victim to hang around and wait for a half an hour please. No one who used to witness the Stalybridge Red[62] Peter Kenyon pushing his trolley around various airports, allegedly in pursuit of Ronaldhino, ever believed he would bring home the Brazilian.

---

61   The BSkyB bid was referred to the Monopolies and Mergers Commission in 1999 but of course the Glazer bid could not receive similar treatment.
62   Despite the moniker he quickly defected to Chelsea. Indeed many of us thought he was already working for Abramovich when he was cocking up United's transfer business. He is credited also in trying to bring Sven Goran Erikson to OT, which at least made Fergie do a U turn.

As a result the Plc Board stood accused periodically of too much stealth or perhaps inertia in its transport dealings – so laid back it was almost horizontal – but that may of course partially at least be the result of the modern market and the high profile of Manchester United. Every chairman in Europe saw them coming and rubbed their hands in glee. The abiding impression of many fans was that, unless Ferguson himself became involved directly in transfer negotiations, they went nowhere fast. Ferguson was often, critically, on holiday during the crucial early months of summer and there is perhaps an argument, once the transfer window came into force that he should have re-adjusted his time off. So many times United fans heard that the high-powered team of Kenyon and Maurice Watkins were jetting off somewhere to do the business. The heart plummets like a stone into a well. You hear it plop as it hits bottom, more or less at the time that Kenyon is seen in the airport, pushing his luggage trolley with a self-satisfied smirk on his face. He thinks he's got his man but the United fan knows the negotiations have bombed again. It's just that he doesn't know it yet. It was almost as if the guy enjoyed it.

Conversely, Kenyon perhaps paid through the nose for some players – Ferdinand is a prime example, although this is a relative thing: Leeds weren't going to sell him immediately after the World Cup for anything less than a reasonable profit on the excessive £18,000,000 they had forked out to West Ham. Unfortunately, publicity over delay in signing a new contract, rumours of excessive demands and a well-publicised meeting with "Tapper" Kenyon, by then suspected of a hidden agenda, appearing to act for United but in fact acting for his Chelsea paymasters, cast doubt over whether the Stalybridge Red was ever as committed to United as he claimed but it can be said that his actions since that unfortunate episode have gone a long way to restoring his credentials.

Whatever the criticisms of Kenyon it cannot be doubted that he proved to be an able and trusting ally of Ferguson, even perhaps at times to the extent of antagonising the Plc paymasters (or were they in truth pay puppets?), doling out vast sums for the likes of Seba Veron, who proved to be an expensive mistake for United and who had the class but probably lacked the bottle to be the complete midfielder in the Premier League. Rio Ferdinand, with whom I have dealt above, and Ruud van Nistelrooy (who was, conversely, cheap at the price and whose place in the United pantheon is guaranteed) were, however, two examples of where he has been vindicated.

To return to the point, however, contrary to the doubters, it seems clear in retrospect that the Glazers must have figured that, if the club could weather the twin hurricanes of a great team in transition and the huge debt with which they had burdened it, there was no reason why they shouldn't do better than their immediate predecessors. There weren't any geniuses in the Boardroom to account for United's unparalled success over the years and the Glazers recognised immediately, therefore, that one man more than any other was responsible for it. We're probably a little nearer, therefore, to solving the puzzle of why United left its rivals behind but certainly not all the way there. What is, however, clear is that, the answer is not to be found in an accumulation of fortunate financial wizardry before the Glazers arrived; it is more likely indeed that the club was in a position to react quickest and best to the new television money coming into football in the early 90's. However, that cannot be said of the post-Glazer period when there suddenly had to be something more than smoke and mirrors to support the club over the debt mountain which the takeover created. In that sense, at least, the owners proved to be the correct one because it was a challenge to which the management now rose.

In order, however, to answer more fully the questions posed in the first chapter it is essential to look back into the company's history to see if there was anything there which might account for its startling rise to prominence in the post-war years and beyond. United's humble beginnings are by now well documented and do not need any remorseless recapitulation here. It is however necessary to examine these briefly in order to try and capture the essence of the post-war rebirth.

CHAPTER 7
MEAN STREETS

I made a point earlier in passing about the inability of German bombers to reduce the club to ruins. It is fair to say that they did however bring about the lowest point of Manchester United history, when the club was banished effectively from playing on its own ground and did not even have the money to rebuild it after the bombing. No one would have thought then that the club would rise so quickly from that disaster but there is a certain irony in it. Those Luftwaffe aces, peering down from their Heinkels and Fokkers and their protective ring of Messerschmitts at their target, the world-famous, pioneering Ship Canal and Europe's first industrial trading estate, must have noticed the football stadium on the fringe of all this industry. Did they have perhaps a flash of déjà vu about what would happen to their most famous football team that May Day in Barcelona's Camp Nou arena?

After all, albeit in a different field of human endeavour, they had exactly the same experience as Matthaus, Effenberg, and Basler *et al* in 1999. The Germans threw everything they had at the red half of Manchester, they had them on the ropes, and they had them down and seemingly out. But they could not land the killer punch. Just as the stadium rose from the ashes of the war and the club with it, bigger and better than ever with Sir Matt at the helm, United, at Barcelona in 1999 famously got back up off the canvas with minutes to go. Like a prize-fighter shaking the concussion from his head, the players then waded in with blow after blow until they shattered German dreams in a heroic ending straight out of the Muhammad Ali *"Rumble in the Jungle"* copybook, with the players of Bayern Munich taking the part of the hapless George Foreman - the rope-a-dope, translated from one arena to another with equally devastating effect.

United started as a football club in 1874, the brainchild of the railway workers of the Lancashire & Yorkshire Railway maintenance department, which was stationed in Newton Heath, so let's deal with the myth that United is not a Manchester Club. Newton is a Manchester Borough. Manchester itself was then part of the Salford Hundred. Records go back at least as far as 1801 when Newton was described as a township in the parish and borough of Manchester. In 1841, when a statistical sketch was carried out by one Edwin Butterworth into the County Palatine of Lancaster, it was described as being on the railway line to Leeds and the canal to Rochdale. In those days it was more or less the extent of the urban limits, stretching eastwards on to the heath.

Newton Heath FC began their playing career in Monsall Road, Newton Heath. If not exactly a pub team, the Heathens, whose badge was a representation of a witch on a broomstick (adapted from a Lancashire railways badge), had no immediate pretensions to fame. Indeed when the first English League came into being in 1882 they felt too humble to apply, among the likes of their near neighbours, Burnley, Bolton and Blackburn, to join this elite. They did join eventually in 1892 and, a decade later, as if deciding that being known by the name of the employer of their original founder members was no longer acceptable in the heady atmosphere of the new and immensely popular Football League, they changed their name. They considered a number of exotic titles before they settled on the rather anodyne 'Manchester United'. Some of the world's clubs have far more expressive, far more romantic names but a rose is a rose, so to speak. The United rose has bloomed hardier than most.

The great majority of the fans who sport the sponsor's shirt today do not really give a fig for United's history. It is nonetheless interesting because it demonstrates that United were once a run-of-the-mill side, no more or less successful than some of the early industrial heartland clubs. The transformation of Football into the universal game, with the rare but now changing exception of the USA,
reflects in many ways the transformation of Manchester United from ugly duckling into majestic swan.

Billy Meredith – the first icon

From inauspicious beginnings the Lancashire railway workers created a team, which, under its new name, started off the new century as it would finish it off and as it would begin the next. The success was intermittent but the first decade of the twentieth century brought promotion from the second division. After a period of consolidation, three trophies came in a row between the start of the 1907-08 season: their first Division I League triumph; the first Charity Shield in 1908; the FA Cup in 1909. Controversy has, however, dogged United's footsteps persistently and the latter was only achieved after the referee called off the quarter-final at Burnley, allegedly because of blizzard conditions, but when United were losing 1-0 (they duly won the replay). Allegedly also the referee, Herbert Bamlett, was so frozen he couldn't blow the whistle so the job fell to one of United's players, Charlie Roberts. You could not make it up!

United's then hierarchy must have found themselves with fond memories of the same Bamlett. When the manager's job became vacant in the late twenties, the ex-ref stepped in, demonstrating a degree of flexibility in the footballing profession which would not have been tolerated in the demarcation philosophy of most of the workers' unions around at that time. It was a shame then that the move from their old ground at Bank Street (the successor to Monsall

Road but controversial for its proximity to a chemical works – they'd have to do the environmental survey these days) to a new stadium at Old Trafford should see them narrowly beaten by the first visitors to that ground. The shame lay not in the 3-4 score line but in the fact that their conquerors that day were Liverpool and thus the second decade started on a downer. It improved when, despite that setback, United went on to triumph for the second time in the League but quickly deteriorated into something far worse, the First World War and a different kind of football match. If Bill Shankly was right when he famously or perhaps apocryphally said that football was much more important than life or death then it is not the way the game was seen back in those days when the onset of hostilities with the aggressive German Empire put it firmly in the shade.

When United returned to football in 1919 it was as if the depression from the war years had not been lifted and the club's fortunes suffered. In fact in the period between the wars United could truly be described as a yo-yo club. Relegated into Division 2 in 1922, getting back in 1925, they performed less than heroically until suffering eventual relegation yet again in 1931. In 1932 the club actually faced bankruptcy. It didn't have the funds to pay the player's wages and, if a Manchester textiles businessman had not invested the then enormous sum of £30,000, the club would have been in the hands of the receivers.[63]

James Gibson's family should have hung on to their shares, although United must have seemed less than a good investment in those days, only just escaping the unthinkable fate of relegation into the Third Division in 1934 after a dog-eat-dog fight with Millwall. The Lions lost and dropped into oblivion. To make things worse, Manchester City won the cup that same week. The man playing right-half would, in just over a decade, transform the fortunes of his opponents on that day and become even more famous in the Red half of Manchester than the Blue. He was Matt Busby.

---

63   The Unseen Archives - A Photographic History of Manchester United: the businessman was James Gibson.

The yo-yoing however continued for United as, achieving the 2nd Division crown in 1936, they returned to the top flight with high hopes, only to be relegated again the next season. The later England manager, Walter Winterbottom, was by then in their ranks. These were bad time because City won the Championship. United came up again in 1938. Johnny Carey came into the team for the first time and they survived in 14th place. Joy of joy, City were relegated. So it goes.

The joy was short-lived. Donner und Blitzen clouds were gathering over Europe and the Europeans had not, by that time, learned to put their leisure interests before the suicide pact of their ruling cartels. In 1939 hostilities with Germany, which had been simmering since the days of the Nazi overthrow of the Weimar Republic, broke like a sudden earthquake. Football went, with the rest of civilised life, on to the back burner. In 1941 the Luftwaffe destroyed Old Trafford. The time of the phoenix had begun.

Before examining why this phoenix flew and perhaps coming up with some prophesy of the future length of the flight it might be appropriate to look at the take-off runway. The history of Association Football gives a perspective to Manchester United as well as to the European game.

In the context of the origins of football, founder membership of the League is not of particular importance. Championship triumphs did not in the early days and, perhaps not until after the Second World War, carry the same kudos as they do now. The FA Cup was seen by many of the early supporters as more important. Certainly it bred the unmistakable atmosphere of excitement which characterises a good cup-tie to this day. In the modern game we have lost a lot of the romance which must have been experienced in these industrial boroughs when the cup circus came to town. Many opposition fans accuse Manchester United of devaluing the FA Cup by the decision to play the FIFA sponsored millennium-based world club championship in Brazil. Tomes have been written about the matter. The world and its dog have had their say. It isn't worth going back over it. The fact is that the FA Cup was devalued. To blame

Manchester United is simply scapegoating, itself an ancient human pastime. The FA, for whatever reasons, wanted United to play in the FIFA tournament. United didn't think the FA Cup was worth standing up for. Who is to blame? What would Arsenal have done, or Liverpool, or Newcastle? They can't answer. They didn't win the Treble, the single act of fulfilment which made United so sought after by football's so called governing body.[64]

The Football League, the predecessor of the present Premiership and Championship Leagues, was founded during a meeting in, yes, Manchester on 23rd March 1888. A number of applications had been received for inclusion in the new league but acceptance of all was impracticable. This didn't prevent a little favouritism taking place. The clubs who initially formed the Football League were Villa, Wolves, Stoke, West Bromwich Albion, Derby County, Notts County, Burnley and Blackburn (Olympia then rather than Rovers). The group was made up to 12 by the invitation of elite teams who had not bothered to turn up, presumably feeling they were indispensable. These were Preston North End, Everton, Bolton Wanderers and Accrington F.C. Wow! In modern terms this is hardly a catalogue of the big hitters.

That isn't, however, the only reason why founder membership of the Football League wasn't that important. There were at least two others. It puts it in context if I say that far and away the best team in the Isles at this point was Queens Park – not Rangers, the Scottish guys. The other (and connected) reason is that this group is a reasonably fair reflection of the clubs which desperately wanted to turn pro. It was a bit like the tennis set up of the 60's. Pressure came down from the hierarchy to remain amateur; demand pushed up from the roots to turn professional and change an increasingly popular spectator sport into hard currency. It is an accepted tenet of business that 'pull' is more effective than 'push'. This is, however, only true of the short term. You may get an early promotion and outstrip your rivals by currying favour with and therefore getting a pull from those above you. Long term you will be found out. Building from the roots

---

64   The debate has been reignited as recently as 14th May 2011. See the Guardian article *The Secret Footballer*

is the only sure-fire philosophy for success.

Football's amateur origins have any number of candidates and it is difficult to pin down any single culprit for the genesis of the game. 'Mob' football has been played in many countries since time immemorial but the Association game certainly began in England in the mid 1800's. In 1863 a group of blokes got together at the Freemason's Tavern on 26th October 1863 to form the Football Association. The only member of that group still playing in the Football League is Crystal Palace. The most famous then was Forest (later to become known as Wanderers), the first winners of the FA Cup. A number of the clubs were formed by Public Schools such as Charterhouse, Blackheath and Kensington.

So, contrary to popular opinion, the origins of the game in England were rooted in the middle classes. They were broadly the same as the origins of cricket and rugby and not much removed from the basis of the game's later development on the continent. The game tends to be seen as much more working class in Britain than it does abroad. This apparent anomaly may of course be explained partly by the fact that the dominant language in football is English and foreign players may therefore appear, from their facility with the English language, to be more intelligent than their English counterparts who have difficulty, sometimes, even talking their own tongue. The fact is of course that footballers are not unusual in this respect. The average salesman selling to the Russians expects them to speak English. It is a legacy of the empire upon which the sun never set and, as with all legacies, it exacted a price from future generations.

The phenomenon of why the continental game evolved differently with something approaching the English concept of 'gentlemen' becoming and staying involved is explained by the fact that the English game was hi-jacked by the northern industrial tribes in the late 1880's. Although the Association game started in the South, particularly in the London area, its development was hamstrung by a number of factors. Firstly, there were far too many disputes between it and the 'handling' game, which eventually became Rugby Union. Secondly, its insistence on amateurism allowed the 'professionals' to steal a march. Thirdly, the proliferation of numerous different interpretations of the 'London Rules' made it difficult for the game ever to break through the barrier which all minority sports have to negotiate at some stage if they are ever to aspire to being a national, let alone a world game.

The simple fact is that by the 1886/87 season the future of the game was very much under the control of the northerners and their no nonsense approach. Down south they might have been playing football for the pleasure of the game but, in a strikingly prophetic evocation of the Liverpool managerial legend, Bill Shankly, the lads from the Bolton mills hadn't come for fun, they'd come to play football. The new diet wasn't easy to swallow for the game's then establishment but it was certainly here to stay. It will not have escaped attention that none among that group of founder members was from the south. The myth of the 'southern softy' began there. Neither, however, was there any representative from further north. No one who has walked up Gallowgate in the depths of a Newcastle winter, among young men in their string vests, has ever accused the Geordies or their cousins, the Mackems, of being 'softies'. Manchester United was not among that (then) northern hard core, nor was Liverpool.

United had been in existence since 1874 in the form of Newton Heath but the club's development was such that in 1888 it did not consider itself of sufficient status to be a founder member of the Football League. The London clubs didn't see fit to take part in the inaugural meetings and the result is that none of those around at the time figure prominently nowadays. Arsenal, by far the most consistently successful of the London clubs, was formed as 'Dial Square' in 1886 by the workers of the Woolwich Arsenal Armanents Factory. Again they were perhaps too plebeian for the establishment clubs of London. Their growing prowess was, however, another indication of the fact that, long before the enfranchisement in voting terms of the lower classes, the workers were taking over the football fields.

The development of those football clubs, which are seen as United's main rivals today, was not markedly different from the Manchester club's. Dial Square, soon to be Royal Arsenal, entered the Football

League in 1893, one year after Newton Heath. After the First World War the English First Division was extended to 22 teams. Arsenal was voted into that elite group. The Gunners are unique in having enjoyed the distinction of never having been out of it since. Whilst United were a yo-yo team between the wars, Arsenal enjoyed their salad days. They were to the First Division of the 30's what United would prove to be in the 90's (and so nearly were in the 50's had it not been for Munich). Arsenal won five league championships in the 30's including one sequence of three in a row and were blessed, because of an astute transfer policy masterminded by Herbert Chapman before his untimely death in 1934, with some spectacular players. Even today the older generation of football supporters has heard of Alex James, Ted Drake and Cliff Bastin, to name but three, who might fairly be described as the Best, Law and Charlton of the pre-war years. After the Second World War Arsenal hit another rich vein of form and took championships and cups in the years either side of the beginning of the 50's, the first decade of United's true greatness. Indeed, the rivalry with Arsenal had its most poignant moment on 1st February 1958 when the team dubbed 'Busby's Babes', because of the comparative callowness of most of its members, beat the Gunners at Highbury by the odd score in a nine goal standoff. Poignant because this was the last time most of the Babes would ever play on English soil.

Entering into the post-war era Arsenal was as well placed as United to take wing. Some will say they have but no one will suggest to the same extent, even since the arrival of the genuinely likeable Arsene Wenger. It was a shame for the Gunners that he seems now as short-sighted as the Cyclops in the way that he has allowed his team to decline since its first decade under his control but he may yet prove more perspicacious than most. The club is financially in a strong position for the next few decades, because of its parsimony of the last, and that should augur well for it in the long term. It just has to rediscover its appetite for coming first, which, once lost, is hard to regain.

Liverpool FC is seen as United's traditional rival, surpassing even Manchester City. This may of course be merely another manifestation of an older rivalry between the two North West cities.

Either way Liverpool is another club with 'history'. Its real glory years span the thirty years or so from 1961 (the date of the club's elevation from the second flight). The Scousers look back fondly on this period as 'the Shankly Revolution' and revolution it was. Liverpool FC's beginnings were comparatively humble in precisely the same way as United's. When the Football League kicked off in 1888 a Liverpool side was not only a founder member but was also playing at home at Anfield. Only it was Everton FC. Some four years later a dispute with the brewer landlord over the rent for the ground made the club up-sticks across Stanley Park and take their ball with them. Left with an area of land fit only for a sports arena or the grazing of livestock, the brewer, John Houlding, decided to form his own football team.

So Liverpool FC was born (Chelsea was formed in 1905 in much the same way when Fulham didn't want to move to Stamford Bridge). Some would say it has never looked back but the truth is of course stranger. Runaway success in the formation years in the Second Division brought the team into the top flight, only for the success to prove a chimera. It returned to the Second in the same season but bounced back and the club's initial First Division championship was secured in 1901 (seven years before United's first triumph in that competition). Indeed Liverpool had won the title twice before United triumphed once – the Anfield team won the League again in 1906. The club was adventurous also in a business sense and was one of the first clubs to expand its ground. The famous Spion Kop (nowadays still fondly known as the Kop, although its metamorphosis is nothing like its original incarnation) was built in those early years. The Liverpool Echo nicknamed the tower of earth and cinders after a hill in South Africa, which had played host to a famous battle between the Boers and the British Army.

After the first world war the Scousers repeated their title triumphs in the 20's but the depression of the 30's hit cities like Liverpool harder than most. The club too became a yo-yo side until in 1947 a Billy Liddell and Bob Paisley inspired side brought the title back to Anfield. Unfortunately, for Manchester's Mersey neighbour, its star waned as United's began to wax. In 1954 Liverpool was relegated with the worst record ever in the First Division. They did not return to the top flight until the Shankly Revolution, one which didn't come to an end, even with the astonishing announcement of the old campaigner's 'retirement' in 1974. The dynasty he had built was like Genghis Khan's, designed to outlast his demise.[65] Even so, the astonishing images of Shankly turning up like a forlorn figure, before his untimely death in 1981, at Everton's training ground, apparently barred from his own club in case he would interfere with its progress, and at Bobby Charlton's home in Cheshire, just to talk about football, is as unedifying for the Merseyside club as it is redolent of the ultimate unscrupulousness of the business end of professional football. One can only contrast it with United's treatment of Matt Busby after his managerial career came to an end. Perhaps the Merseysiders perceived that Busby had continued, after his retirement, to cast a long shadow over Old Trafford and there was no fear of their allowing that to happen at Anfield. If so it was the kind of Machiavellian stance which Shankly might have appreciated, had he not been its victim. His was a clear case of living and dying by the sword. Even before one begins to look at Liverpool's unprecedented era of achievement under Shankly and his successors, Paisley, Fagan and King Kenny, it isn't hard to see that, entering into the post-war era, the club was a candidate for England's version of top dog at the millennium, when Real Madrid was awarded its 'world' prize.

Thus, their two arch-rivals in pole position, United were lagging well behind at the beginning of that period - they didn't even play at their own ground - and a gulf opened up between them and the other two (particularly Liverpool) in the 70's and 80's. How, therefore, after Munich and even allowing for Liverpool's (and to a lesser extent Arsenal's) success in the period through from the 70's to the millennium, did the century end with a United side towering so high in global popularity terms above both? The easy answer of course is

---

65 Unlike Busby's, for whom the effort of creating a third great side had proved too much for him to leave anything for his successor, although much of that may have to do with the lasting effects of the near-death experience of Munich. Sammy McIlroy also was to be damned with the title of the 'last of the babes'. Perhaps the greatest casualty was Brian Kidd, who, when he emerged in 1968, looked a world-beater but, deprived of colleagues of similar status, found his summer flowering had turned all too quickly into a dark winter's decline. In this way, it is easy to see the condemnation of United to years in the wilderness, whilst still building an astonishing world-wide fan base, as the final legacy of Munich.

Munich and it may well be part of the truth. But is it all? For instance, the Italian Club, Torino, suffered a terrible aeroplane crash in 1949[66] but has been eclipsed by its Turin neighbour, Juventus.[67] A plane crash, in which a great young team dies, is not therefore a guarantee of immortality.

---

66   The Torino plane crash was on 4th May 1949 whilst descending into Turin en route from Lisbon. 31 people including 18 players were killed. The club fielded its youth side for the remaining four matches of the season and still won the *Scudetto* largely because their opponents were gracious enough to field their youth sides also.

67   The club is known as *La Vecchia Signora (the old lady)* and also as *La Fidanzata diItalia (the girlfriend of Italy)* it is slightly older than Torino FC. Indeed it was playing in its traditional black and white stripes, based on the Notts County strip, from three years before Torino was born (see the respective club websites). It came to prominence very probably because of its (partially immigrant) support from the Fiat automobile works. However, until 1949 Torino had a pretty well matchless record in Italian football.

CHAPTER 8
FOREIGN FIELDS

Talk of some of the great European giants leads on to the fact that, in trying to get to grips with the reason why a team like United enjoys such international standing, it would be wrong to compare it only with its domestic rivals. The 'usual suspects' in Ferguson's words of the modern European game are to be identified as Real Madrid and Barcelona of Spain, Juventus and the two Milan clubs of Italy, together with Bayern Munich and Ajax Amsterdam. Others regularly tag on to the coat tails of Ferguson's select group without ever actually acquiring the qualification to join it. Those seven are the continental teams, which qualify for the Champions' League time and time again with only the odd blip and will continue to do so probably for as long as the modern game now retains its popularity.

In the 1990's United was initially the only English, or indeed British club, to sit at the top table with those august colleagues.[68] Once it was Liverpool. Arsenal is regularly to be found knocking at the door, asking for an invitation, but the London club is not really part of the elite group even though it has never failed to qualify for the Champions League since the latter ceased to be the sole preserve only of the champions of the various member leagues. Chelsea has proved itself a contender over the last few years and Manchester City will over the next few. The other Manchester club may find itself in a similar situation to AC Milan for a time. Berlusconi's media money bought the older Milan club the players, particularly the Dutch trio of Gullit, Rijkard and Van Basten, who would win them *Scudettos* and European Cups during a purple passage in the late eighties. These foreign giants certainly did not, however, sweep all before them immediately after their formation as will be seen

---

68   The G14 elite group of clubs was formed in 2000 and included Liverpool. It was later expanded to 18 and then also included Arsenal. It wasn't perhaps intended to reflect this regular qualification for European tournaments but certainly derived from it because it was a club v country group in effect and it never included such large newcomers as Chelsea or City. It was disbanded in 2008 when it reached an international appearances compensation agreement with FIFA.

from a brief historical perspective.

The game on the continent evolved differently from the British game. If the northern clubs were at least a good decade behind their London counterparts, the continental clubs were a generation adrift. Most of these clubs may well have looked to Britain as the model for their own creation but there is not a great deal of evidence of an evangelical movement. British clubs didn't start showing the flag on any regular basis until the beginning of the 20th Century. Indeed, the first recorded tour abroad by a club from Britain was in 1890 from Clapton FC! Queens Park (the one in Glasgow) went to Copenhagen in 1898 and 1900. Surrey Wanderers (as their name implies) were seasoned travellers and toured Geneva, Lausanne and Zurich in 1900 followed by Den Haag, Vienna, Prague and Budapest in 1901. Aston Villa played a Germany 11 in Berlin in 1901. Celtic went to Vienna and Prague in 1904. Chelsea followed suit and added Copenhagen in 1906. Arsenal went ambitiously to Brussels, Den Haag, Berlin, Prague, Vienna and Budapest in 1907. United went to the latter three in 1908 and Liverpool had its first tour (Gothenburg, Stockholm and Copenhagen) in 1914. It was the footballing equivalent of the European "Grand Tour" which was very British and aristocratic in origin and started in about 1660.[69]

Of the foreign clubs there is no better place to start than in Madrid. Real Madrid FC started off the new century as if it meant to claim the accolade of this century's greatest team to go with that of last. A lot can of course happen in the course of a century,[70] as the history of Manchester United shows, but this most elitist of Spanish teams, which proudly declares itself to be 'the best club in history', has led a fairly charmed life. It is surprising, therefore, that, despite its modern aspirations to global supremacy, it cannot claim a fan base anything like the equivalent of Manchester United's.[71] The superlative 'best' is not, however, undeserved in terms of its achievement on the field and has, in any event, been given official

---

69   See e.g Thompson *The Making of the English Working Class* 1991.

70   Or indeed the first decade or so as Barcelona went on to show. See below.

71   The Real Madrid fan base is estimated at circa 450m to Man United 50m but it has to be admitted tha t it depends whose stats you read. These come from Siemens and Forbes respectively.

blessing by the FIFA declarations of 12th January 1998 ('the best club in history' with Alfredo Di Stefano as 'the best player') and of 23rd December 2000 ('the best club of the 20th Century'). Di Stefano, rather fittingly, collected the latter award on behalf of the club. It is perhaps rather fittingly ironic that, within a decade of that accolade, its arch-rival, FC Barcelona, would, in the same frenzy of hyperbole, be acclaimed as the greatest football team ever.[72]

Real, like United in England, is nothing like the oldest club in Spain. That honour belongs to a little-known club called Recreativo de Huelva. It was formed by English mineworkers working at Tharsis. Thus, the English taught the Spaniards the game of football and, some would say, they have been taking lessons from the pupil ever since. Three years after the foundation of Barcelona by a Swiss sportsman called Hans Gamper, an employee of a French Bank which had an office in the Catalan city, Real was formed in 1902 as Madrid Football Club by a group of Spanish football enthusiasts. Its international credentials were, however, already to the fore: the club adopted its famous white strip in imitation of London's Corinthians (one of the remaining English amateur clubs). Fittingly, also, its first coach was an Englishman, Arthur Johnson. The Spaniards were paying homage to the English game but it was perhaps more the remnants of the London Rules game than the grittier professional game of the industrial north and west midlands.

Madrid was instantly successful, its first Spanish championship coming in 1905. It won five more before the First World War and gained the prefix 'Real' in 1920 by gift from an enraptured King. In the same year, it undertook its first foreign tour (of Portugal and Italy). In 1926 the club toured England, Denmark and France and in 1927 the continent of America. In 1931 it won the League without losing a game.

Just as the Second World War would later set United's ambitions back a number of years, so the Spanish Civil War between 1936 and 1939 took a devastating toll on Real Madrid. Its pitch had been used as a prisoner-of-war camp and was in ruins. The club had to start

---

72 See e.g Back Page Football 28th February 2011.

more or less from scratch. One of the club's legendary players became its president and work began on the stadium which is named after him, the Santiago Bernabeu. Rather more controversially, the team's situation in Madrid meant that it was adopted by the dubious circle of cronies which surrounded the bloody Fascist dictator, General Franco. Its tag as the brutal dictator's club of choice has never really been lived down among non-Madridistas. By contrast Barcelona is seen as a distinctly Catalan rather than Spanish club and as the embodiment in some respects of the Republican resistance to fascism.[73]

By the time of its fiftieth anniversary the Madrid club had recovered sufficiently to host and take part in an international tournament. Ironically, in light of subsequent history, one of the visiting teams was so special that it was dubbed 'The Millionaires'. It was a representative team from South America. The visitors' outstanding player was one Alfredo di Stefano. One is tempted at this point to say nothing more than the rest is history. It is not only in modern times that the philosophy of the Madrid club has been, "if we can't beat you, you can join us."

The European Cup began in 1956. Madrid won the first on 13th June of that year and its experienced side was too much for the Babes in their 1957 semi-final. That April night is still described by the Madrid club as 'the biggest battle in our history'. It was just one battle in what was expected to become a friendly war for supremacy. Another battle was looming in 1958 but of course, by then, the friendly war was already over as a result of an act of God.

Real went on to win the next three Cups in a row, the last one in 1960 a 7-3 victory against Eintracht Frankfurt in what has often been called the best ever European Cup Final. Thus the Madrid players cemented their reputation as the top club in the world. From that moment the top club's decline was rapid, despite another victory in the Champions' Cup in 1966 by its so-called 'Hippy' side. The

---

[73] Historically, after its Roman or perhaps Carthaginian roots (it is purported by some to be named after Hamilcar Barca although the name may in fact derive from the even older Phoenician *Barkeno*), the city was part of the Crown of Aragon rather than Castile. The forging of an alliance between the two Crowns marked its decline and Madrid's pre-eminence, which is resented to this day.

club's only other appearance in the final before its recent return to hegemony was in 1981 when Liverpool won 2-0. Real's current dominance began in 1998 and in the early noughties it was almost taken for granted that the club would win the Champions' Cup every year because of its policy of buying, at the end of each season, the world's number one player. Two of those were of course United's own David Beckham, who, despite many detractors, did not look at all out of place in Madrid's pantheon, and Cristiano Ronaldo, who is possibly the biggest star ever even in its firmament.[74] Of course that grand plan did not work out and there were no successes between 2002 and 2014, an era during which Barcelona won the cup three times and Manchester United appeared in the final on three occasions, triumphing once. Even Liverpool and Porto managed wins in those seasons.

It is a fair point, even if one accepts the view is one observed through rose-tinted spectacles, that the Munich air crash made Real Madrid the best team in the world. Its ageing stars might have defeated United again in 1958 but I much doubt it. The tide of history was with United. In defeat Madrid would have regrouped and re-bought (the current *galacticos* policy has in fact been the club's *modus operandi* in one guise or another for over half a century and, bearing in mind the manner in which it earned its *Real* title, probably longer) so I do not say that United would definitely have won the cup again in 1959 and 1960 but that young side was yet to reach its peak. As the money flowed into the coffers, there can be little doubt that Busby would have taken a leaf out of Santiago Bernabeu's book and strengthened in key departments. Certainly the trophy was easier to win in those days, because there were very few matches. One thing is certain: the sad events of that frozen Munich runway deprived the world's growing football community of a spectacle.

---

74   Whilst it was perhaps inevitable that Cristiano would go (and he has been rewarded in 2014 with a second ECL triumph) it was by no means necessary for Beckham to go. Indeed it did no one any real good. Cristiano would still have come to United.

10 years after Munich (1968)

Staying in Spain for the moment, the slightly more elderly Barcelona was, at least before the late noughties, an underachiever by comparison but significantly its best period came when Real's star waned. The Catalan club has always given the impression that, like United, it stands for something more than merely football. It is in effect the focal point of a people which perceives itself as being independent of the Madrid based (and dominated) Republic. These political undertones were of far greater importance in the days of the Fascist dictatorship when Real was seen to take the benefit of the dictator's particular brand of favouritism. Even though all that should have changed with the new Republic, there are, no doubt, many in Catalonia who feel that the area from the Pyrenees south should be its own master. Barcelona, the city and the club, is a sort of standard bearer for a dream of a free Catalan province.[75] Perhaps

---

75   The Catalan referendum on independence from Spain was planned for 9th November 2014 but cancelled after opposition from Madrid.

the club therefore used to measure its own achievements negatively by the extent to which it could dent Real Madrid's ambitions but its successes in the early years of the new millennium have changed that perspective. There is a new pride afoot in the Catalan city.

Barca's early history was relatively anonymous compared to Real's. It was, however odd it may now seem, the Spanish team most notorious for fielding foreign players. Although famous in Spain and well-known in European competitions down the years, the club didn't really take off until Johann Cruyff signed in 1973. It won the League that year and then enjoyed a golden era but still only managed to win its first European Cup (with Cruyff back as manager) in 1992, one year after losing to United in an epic European Cup Winners' Cup Final.

The other immediate beneficiary of the Munich air crash was AC Milan, the club which effectively took United's place in the 1958 final. Relative newcomers on the European scene it has become since the competition's second greatest achievers. Founded by Englishmen, diplomat and socialite, Alfred Edwards, and Herbert Kilpin in 1900 as the Milan Cricket and Football Club it is not hard to see that Italy's principal city was captivated by the English sporting obsession.

Originally the club had both a footballing and a cricketing division but no one remembers much of the cricket. The original football team was a mixture of local and British players and the club quickly won its first title in 1901 eclipsing at that stage the more famous Genoa. The club's name Associazone Calcio Milan, was dropped in 1919 for the mere Milan Football Club but it was restored under the Fascists in 1938. Apart from dropping the 'o' of Milano the club retained the name long after the demise of Mussolini. The club has always worn the famous red and black colours, allegedly the brainchild of Herbert Kilpin who is supposed famously to have said "let us be like the devil and instil fear in everyone"[76]. The club's nickname the *Rossoneri* derives of course from these colours as does Inter Milan's *Nerazurri*.

---

76   FIFA.com AC Milan Website

AC Milan grew of course to be the most successful club in Italian history in the European Cup, having had greater success than any club other than Real Madrid and even greater success in the modern era than the Spanish giants. It has won the European Cup seven times between 1963 and 2007 whereas five of Madrid's ten triumphs came in the first five years of the trophy when, after the Munich air crash, it went effectively unchallenged for four years. All of Milan's successes came when the trophy was more fiercely contested. The club has also won eighteen *Scudettos*, the Italian League title, but its fortunes declined after its 2007 European Champions League triumph over Liverpool FC.

Milan's other major club, Internaziole, was formed in 1908 by a group of rebels from the Milan Club. Its stated aim was to encourage enlistment among foreign players as well as native-born Italians. The club's formative colours of gold, black and blue remain to this day. Again success was almost instantaneous, the club gaining its first League win in 1910. Just as Tottenham Hotspur was once famous for winning a trophy in the first year of each new decade, Inter repeated its *Scudetto* triumphs in 1920, 1930 and 1940. By the time of the latter achievement it was, like Real Madrid, a Fascist controlled club operating under the odd name of Ambrosiano Inter. As far as I know the club's political past has never been held against it but it is fair to say that the revolution which brought Mussolini to power was relatively bloodless and of course his overthrow was little more than a bloody vignette in a time of immense turmoil.[77] Internaziole also won League titles in 1938, 1939 and 1953 and 1954. In 1963 under Hellenio Herrera the club began its domination of Italian football, winning *Scudettos* in 1964 through1966. It took up the baton falling from Real's faltering hand by winning European Cups in 1964 (against Real) and 1965 (against Benfica). Its much criticised '*cattanaccio*' style of play was not good enough however to overcome Glasgow Celtic's 'Lisbon Lions' in 1967. That defeat heralded the end of Inter's golden era and many would say it has

---

77 Defeated in the vote at the Grand Council of Fascism on 24th July 1943, the dictator was incarcerated and then freed by German special forces. Attempting to escape north in April 1945 he was executed summarily by his own countrymen. His body was hung upside down at a service station in Milan as proof of his demise.

been a stark winter. Although the club frequently appears among Ferguson's 'usual suspects', it has not achieved much in Europe's highest tournament since and the *coup de grace* has more than once been delivered by its neighbour and bitter rival.[78]

No talk of Italian football is complete without mentioning the third and possibly greatest member, in terms of consistency, of its triumvirate of great sides. Juventus, as the name implies, was formed in 1900 by a group of students from the *Liceo D'Azeglio* in Turin. The youngsters had time on their hands and wanted to form a sports club along the lines of the then established British model. The club's distinctive pink shirts bore witness to the fact that Juve started for fun! Even so the players were sufficiently serious to win their first League title in 1905 (by which time the club had changed to its familiar black and white stripes, allegedly as a result of the English manufacturer sending the wrong consignment of shirts).

After that they team's various players did little to distinguish themselves until after the First World War when, in 1923, the Agnelli family acquired the club. In 1926 the second championship arrived. Five followed consecutively in the first years of the 1930's. Thus, Juve was the Arsenal of Italy but it also took part in those years in the Europe Cup (a forerunner of the 1955-56 competition) and reached the semi-finals four times without ever claiming the crown, a sad tradition of underachievement which would dog its future footsteps.

The 1950's saw Juve triumph in the domestic league in 1950 and 1952, then (with the Welsh 'gentle giant' John Charles in the team) in 1958, 1960 and 1961. In 1961 it was the first club to wear the special star awarded to winners of ten *Scudettos* (the earliest triumphs apparently not counting for this purpose). Winning the *Scudetto* again in 1967 the club went on a long and largely uninterrupted triumphal march until 1986, winning nine more domestic championships and the European Cup in the ultimately tragic victory over Liverpool at Heysel in 1985. The players who

---

[78] Its win over Bayern Munich in 2010 being its one triumph of the modern era. The triumph was masterminded by Jose Mourinho and the style wasn't far removed from *catanaccio*.

received a winners' medal that day might not agree with me but this was one match which should not have been played.

Under the regime of Marcello Lippi the club returned to its successful past and repeated its European Cup triumph in 1996, losing the same tournament in 1997 (to Borussia Dortmund, somewhat fortunate conquerors of United in the semi-final), 1998 (Real Madrid) and 2003 (AC Milan) whilst, on the first occasion at least, being the overwhelming favourite. All in all Juve is the most consistent of the Italian members of the usual suspects.

It is probably not appropriate to pass on from the city of Turin without mentioning Torino, the other Turin side. In Britain at least, in the 60's, Torino was more famous than its neighbour. This was probably because the club bought Denis Law from Manchester City and he was the English game's then MVP. It was equally famous for having subsequently sold him to Matt Busby's post-Munich Manchester United for the then record British fee of £115,000. As previously pointed out, Torino should also be mentioned in the context of this book in order to disprove the hypothesis, sometimes raised in respect of Manchester United's success, that the Munich tragedy turned it into a great football team. Torino too suffered an air-crash in 1949. Eighteen of its team members perished, many of whom were full internationals. The heart was ripped out of the Italian side just as it would be out of the England team immediately before the 1958 World Cup, the one in which Pele, not Duncan Edwards, became world-famous. Both club and country in each case underwent a revival but A.S Torino has not become a phoenix. The club has not taken flight in the Italian, let alone the European or the world, popular imagination. As the Old Trafford song goes of City, so in Turin could the Old Lady's fans be forgiven for singing of their rivals, "nobody knows your name."

To complete the identikit of the usual suspects of European and, therefore, of world football it would be wrong not to mention the other regular top table diners. Bayern Munich was also formed in that seminal year of 1900 by a Berliner called Franz John who got together with a group of friends to create the club. By 1920 Bayern was Munich's biggest club. The German game was in its formative years organised on a regional basis. However, Bayern won its first national title in a 1932 playoff against Eintracht Frankfurt. It was not really, however, until 1972 that the club achieved domination in Germany, winning three titles from 1972-1974 and adding to that a hat-trick of triumphs in the European Cup between 1974 and 1976.

Ajax Amsterdam was also officially founded in 1900 (although it owes its origins to 1883, the name FC Ajax itself coming into existence in 1894). The traditional colours of red and white were adopted almost immediately after the club's formation and the club rules drawn up in April 1893 exhort the players to 'provide pleasant and healthy entertainment'. Exactly how high was the standard is difficult now to know. Suffice it to say that it drew once and was beaten twice between 1909 – 1911 by Man U. No, not United, but Manchester University. Apparently British students, too, were good, competitive footballers in those days!

Even Ajax's detractors at PSV and Feyenoord would scarcely deny that the club has lived up to that pledge in its rules. It then enjoyed some early triumphs in the Amsterdam Golden Cross tournament but its first national ambitions were realised in the period from 1929 – 1939. Ajax won the league championship seven times in that period and the national championship (the Cup) five times. In the period from 1971 to 1973 the club came out of the blue to achieve European domination, winning the European Cup three times in succession.

Ajax's success can be put down to a Matt Busby like figure, Rinus Michels, its inspirational coach and Johann Cruyff, at the time widely rated as the best player in the world. When he left for Barca in 1973 Ajax disappeared back into a Dutch shell for a time. A group of Dutch footballers who, for years to come, would be recognised as components of the best international side in the world (even though they did not win either World Cup final in which they played) lost their talisman. The club, however, returned to success with this prodigal son's return in 1981.

Finally, in the Louis Van Gaal era of 1991 – 1997[79] Ajax won a fourth European Cup (in 1995 against AC Milan) and narrowly lost the 1996 final to Juve on penalties. Like Bayern and Manchester United Ajax has achieved its successes with largely home-grown sides. The club has been in many ways a victim of its own success in that regard. As commercial interests began to dominate football its greatest talents like Cruyff and, later, Marco van Basten and Patrick Kluivert, were tempted away to greener pastures. They assisted in winning many trophies for their paymasters in Spanish and Italian football.

The experiences of those famous clubs, therefore, demonstrates that the development of the game on the continent was generally quite gentlemanly, owing more to the origins of the English game than to its later working-class manifestation when the industrial north and midlands of England got it by the scruff of the neck. This is probably reflected today in the apparent urbanity and linguistic flexibility of the average Serie A or Bundesliga footballer compared with his dourer English counterpart.

The development of the game in this country has meant that it remains generally one for working-class heroes. On the continent it has a more cosmopolitan *afficianado*. The fan base in this country is perhaps changing as the money pours into the game but not so the grass roots and in this, as in so many other things in the domestic game, none epitomises the working class ethos more than Manchester United. The club from the famous machine shop of the north has a fan base which is profoundly working class and proud of it, despite the global fame of the club.

What is more to the point, however, is that there is little in the blueprint of even 'the usual suspects' which gives any clue as to why the proletarian team from the industrial heartland of England should have shown them such a clean pair of heels, if not necessarily in terms of success on the football field, then certainly in global prominence as the profile of the game improved the world over.

---

79   It is testament to this manager's longevity that in 2010 he would coach Bayern Munich to a losing final (Internaziole Milan) and would still be appointed manager of United for the 2014 - 2015 season.

CHAPTER 9
THE CRUSADERS

All of the clubs we have mentioned, whether domestic or continental, have had a greater opportunity (on the basis that none has suffered anything similar by way of setback) than Manchester United to rise to the top of the tree. All have done so with more or less success on the only field of comparison, the European arena, but none, not even Real Madrid, has managed to rival United in terms of global popularity. Real and more recently Barcelona are belatedly making that push and seem to have the savvy and financial clout to put themselves on the leader board but the others are lagging well behind. Why is that? Particularly as United has had to reinvent itself from abnormal tragedies in sporting terms not once but twice.

Of the usual suspects there can be no doubt that Real Madrid's accumulation of ten European Cup wins[80] marks it out as the greatest achiever in that competition and therefore worthy of the title of the greatest football team ever. Theirs is the standard by which every team measures itself. None aspires ever to beat the Madrid club's record in that competition, much of which was achieved when it was a fledgling trophy and easier to win than it would become after 1960. That isn't of course the end of the matter because Real has won the trophy four times in the last sixteen years. It simply means that its early hegemony is misleading and it cannot now consider itself in a class of its own either on the continent or indeed domestically. By no means does it have things all its own way in Spain and over the last few years Madrid has had to play second fiddle to a Barcelona team which has twice beaten Manchester United in European Champions League finals in 2009 and 2011 and is considered by many to be the finest club side ever.[81]

If the European Cup was Matt Busby's Holy Grail, it soon became

---

[80] The latest was of course the 2014 triumph in the only ever city derby final against *Atletico Madrid*. The others are 1998 (Juventus), 2000 (Valencia) and 2002 (Bayer Leverkusen).
[81] Even in 2014 they couldn't manage higher than third in *La Liga*.

Alex Ferguson's too. Indeed, one got the impression in the early days that the junior Glaswegian was unlikely to settle until he had won it twice and therefore eclipsed Busby's achievement.[82] Remaining true to my thesis that Munich robbed United of its greatest period of triumph, however, Busby should now be so far out of sight, both in terms of European Cups and domestic trophies that Sir Alex would have to settle for trailing honourably in his fellow Scot's wake. Sir Matt's legacy would be a yardstick, an achievement to aspire to, but he would have accepted when taking the job that the chances of ever repeating it would be all but non-existent for precisely the same reason that no team can aspire to erase Real's record from the books. Times are very much harder now.

The European Cup started in the 1955/1956 season. Perhaps prophetically, in view of events at Stamford Bridge these days, Chelsea won its only First Division Championship that season but the FA would not permit the club to enter into the continental competition. Why this was the case is not entirely clear because the myth of the English being far better than their foreign counterparts had already been shattered by the 'Magical Magyars' at Wembley in 1953 and in the Nep stadium in Budapest in 1954 (aggregate 13-4). Nonetheless there was an element of xenophobia about the FA's attitude, echoed perhaps in the League Secretary Alan Hardaker's unforgettable and, in today's politically correct climate, near unprintable words, if they had not been historically accurate, that continental football was full of "too many wogs and dagoes".

One might have thought such attitudes would have undergone a sea change after the FA, in 1950, finally relented and let England play in the World Cup (resulting in the ignominious defeat by the all but non-footballing USA). It seems such ignorance dies hard and it does have its mitigating factors in the proximity of these times to the Second World War when Britain perceived itself as having stood alone to preserve the sort of freedom which Hardaker's attitude was in fact undermining. Even England's World Cup hat-trick hero, Geof Hurst, admitted that in 1966 it was hard for the players to put anti-German sentiments out of their minds. Perhaps no harder than it was,

---

82   He achieved this against Chelsea in 2008.

even later, for the Germans to forget their island enemies, for the perceived injustice of that goal! Of course Manchester United and particularly the charismatic and visionary Matt Busby were having nothing of such die-hard bigotry. Whether that was the result of a superior enlightenment or merely of footballing ambition I leave others to judge.

There were probably some smug as well as devastated faces in FA boardrooms when the news came through on 6th February 1958 of the death of a team which might well have dented Real Madrid's early monopoly of the European trophy. Although the Spaniards, with at least one of those Magical Magyars in their side (Puskas), bested the young Reds in the 1957 semi-final, the jury was out on whether the result of the 1958 Final would be the same. The football world's majority thought it was the English team's time. The clash of the titans was certainly going to happen. AC Milan, who beat the post-Munich United reserves in the semi-final that year and duly went on to be Real Madrid's latest victims, would not have withstood the blooming of the flower of Manchester who perished in the crash. Its players were singularly unconvincing in overcoming United's cobbled together second string.

We will never know of course what the outcome would have been of a 1958 Real – United final and history is full of what ifs. However, the impression remains that the younger Manchester side would have overhauled an ageing Madrid team possibly as early as 1958, definitely by 1959 or 1960. Consequently it isn't hard to make a case for the claim that Munich robbed United of a possible hat-trick of European Cups. It would not have been surprising for this side to have achieved such unprecedented success. The Babes were long accustomed to reaching and going beyond milestones. This was the team which won the FA Youth Cup five times on the trot between 1953 – 57. 30,000 spectators turned out to see them play the second leg of the final against Wolves at Molineux in 1954. In the same year those same young men played for the first time in a European Youth Tournament in Switzerland. They won all seven matches, scoring 21 to 2 against. It was inevitable from the moment they marked their arrival in the European Cup with a 10 – Nil win over Anderlecht that this group was going to leave an equally impressive mark on Europe.

Thus, Real Madrid was the beneficiary, as much as Bolton Wanderers (in the 1958 Cup Final) and Wolves, Burnley and Spurs in the domestic game, of the weakening of Manchester United after the Munich plane crash. Even in 1958 the world wanted to see the Babes. Real Madrid might have won the two European Cups since the inauguration of the tournament but United's youthful team had already captured the imagination of a football world, which appreciated, as if with a kind of sixth sense, that the game had begun the process of its transformation into a global phenomenon. In the quarter-finals in that fateful year the citizens of the deprived and dilapidated Iron Curtain city of Belgrade lined the freezing streets, many of them in shoes fashioned from tyre rubber, and chanted, in defiance of their totalitarian governors and ruthless armed police, for the 'Busby Babes', for the 'Red Devils'. United was recognised as prophets not only in their own country but also in the most hostile and politically impenetrable of foreign lands. In a few short hours those same players would be mourned worldwide as an immortal symbol of youth sacrificed on the altar of a cruel providence. And there lies the key to their immortality and the continued popularity of the club. United is, like so many who fell in the world wars, the symbol of Britain's, perhaps more specifically England's, doomed youth. *Dulce et decorum est pro patria mori.*[83]

Thus, Munich might have enhanced but did not give life to the legend of Manchester United. It was already there. It started just after the Second World War when Matt Busby and the tough-talking Welshman, Jimmy Murphy, took over the management of the club. The achievements of the club under an inspirational captain in Johnny Carey in the 40's brought glamour back into lives long brutalised by two generations of world wars. The rise of a largely home-grown team in the 50's which might well carry all in the world before it, the Munich disaster and its aftermath, played out before the eyes of the whole word in a German hospital, only added the ingredients from which the spirit of romance is made. The fighting

---

83 Wilfred Owen's poem of the same name lamented the patriotism of both sides in the Great War.

qualities shown by the team in the aftermath of Munich and the near canonisation of the greatest player of his generation, Bobby Charlton, simply boiled the mix up into a marvellously rich stew upon which the fans and the media alike would feast when the club returned to its cavalier roots and set off to conquer Europe again in the 60's.

Matt Busby and his football philosophy created United's national profile and put the club on the launch pad for international success. The serendipitous arrival of the Busby Babes fostered this spirit of romance by giving Manchester and the nation a group of young gods to whom they could look up in the bleak decade after the Second World War. Munich gave the legend lift off. The slaughter of the young gods by an impervious providence was the stuff of tragic myth.

As with the death of all gods the story is not complete until the rebirth. It is winter and spring. It was not however easy. Ken Ramsden, a long time United employee, remembers that when he joined the club in 1960 as an office boy, "there was no money in the club at all .... In those days the club was very poor .... You really had to make a strong case for buying anything at all ... it was make do and mend... the war had only been over for fifteen years and while lots of people came through the turnstiles, gate receipts were not high. So there wasn't a great deal of money swirling round ..."[84] It was as well they found enough to purchase Denis law from Torino in 1961.

Manchester United was finally reborn after Munich with the fabulous trinity of Best, Law and Charlton. They were not of course the only players of that era. Bill Foulkes, another Munich survivor, would play his part, as would the Munich hero, Harry Gregg. Noel Cantwell would arrive from West Ham and the catalyst would eventually be Paddy Crerand's capture from Celtic. His almost telepathic understanding with Denis Law was instrumental in the Lawman's goal scoring feats of the 60's. It was Law and Charlton, however, who carried the myth until the legend was then personified

---

84   United We Stand – Graham McColl 2002 (page 129).

in George Best, a young, handsome Irishman who hit town just about at the point when the Sixties were getting into Swing.

The Comeback – the 1966/67 League winning team

With the fairy tale ending of the European Cup in May 1968 the club made the hyper leap into outer space. It needed all that altitude to keep it in the mind's eye because the voyage back to 'The Promised Land' was as perilous as anything Captain Kirk and the crew of the Enterprise had to put up with. However, the course was set fair when the Trinity was replaced by the Quartet. United's reincarnation of the Busby Babes with its "Class of 92" brought back the magic and the 'hunger' was finally satisfied on that night in Barcelona, 26th May 1999. To be there was something special, a reminder, in less fraught circumstances of course, of Shakespeare's words in *Henry V*.[85]

Many of us could have spoken in such terms as we scoured Barcelona that night for any company, which would talk at length of

---

85   I am thinking of: *We few, we happy few, we band of brothers.For he today that sheds his blood with meShall be my brother; be he ne'er so vile,This day shall gentle his condition.And gentlemen in England now abedShall think themselves accursed they were not here,And hold their manhoods cheap whiles any speaksThat fought with us upon Saint Crispin's day."*

the match. And it wasn't hard to find, whether Catalans jealous that Louis Van Gaal's team had not emerged from the Group of Death (as had United and Bayern) to contest the final in their own capital; or the remnants of the Southern German army, still in shell-shock from the manner of their club's last gasp defeat but generally sporting for all that. The way the Catalans felt was much as United fans must have on another memorable day in 2003, when, after getting the best of a 4 – 3 against the *galacticos* of Real Madrid, the team went out of the Champions League in a year when the final was to be played on home turf. This was an Old Trafford night when the Brazilian Ronaldo scored a hat-trick but still ended up on the losing side (but not on aggregate). The realisation set in that it was others and not United who would contest the final that year at Old Trafford. These were missed opportunities, just as was the year earlier when a cup final against the same Real Madrid at Hampden Park seemed there for the taking, only to be dashed on away goals by the comparative minnows of Bayer Leverkusen.

After that triumph, which was as much for the country as for the club, bearing in mind how long Britain had been starved of a winner of this competition, the club got very little assistance from the FA. It started with the withdrawal from the third round of the FA Cup, which the FA left with United as if it was the club's decision alone, whereas it was clear that the FA wanted United to take on this assignment before the media tongues started to wag about devaluation of the FA Cup. Things got worse from there and it was as if the club was being punished for its success, for its hubris.

The vendetta the FA appeared to have against United at this time was difficult to understand and one might be forgiven for relating it back in an ironic way to that Alan Hardaker sentiment that the club was too big for its boots. The shameful treatment of Rio Ferdinand was a case in point. He was punished with a lengthy ban for forgetting to take his drugs test. Compared with similar punishments in this country for the same offence with scarcely less mitigation, this looked like a strike at Manchester United. How a club with the pedigree of Manchester City could tell Christian Negouai that it was okay to slip out and collect his mum from the airport and come back and take his test later, was difficult enough to credit but the forgiveness shown to him by the FA for this lapse was staggering when compared with the treatment of Ferdinand. Didn't the club have a driver they could have sent? Negouai's offence wasn't one of forgetfulness; it was much more wilful than Rio's and was aided and abetted by his club but the FA's excuse was that he was not a role model, he was not a high profile player.

What arrant nonsense! What they meant is he didn't play for Manchester United. Does anybody out there seriously believe that if he had been a Red, even one in the reserve team, he would have got away with a £2,000 fine? Equally, the lenient punishments handed out and condoned in Europe for actual offences defied belief when compared with the Draconian punishment which Ferdinand received. There appeared to be an element here of cutting Manchester United down to size. United's approach didn't help and was misconceived by the club's lawyers, which was surprising when they had someone of the pedigree of Maurice Watkins on the Board. Their instinct was, initially, to fight when they should have seen it as a fight they could not win outright. If they couldn't win it outright they should have sued for peace and lived to fight another day.

They should have put their hands up, accepted a ban for the player and got on with it without him. I for one believe that the season would have worked out differently. It was no doubt the sense of injustice which inflamed the situation, the fact that the FA leaked the scandal to the media, and the refusal to allow Rio to complete a test belatedly at a time when it should have been possible to prove one way or the other if he was guilty of taking performance enhancing drugs.

United's officials allowed themselves to fall into the trap of a charge of arrogance and suddenly the FA had the moral high ground. The media circus after that was astonishing. The FA made a mockery of itself with its long-drawn out media trial and then its internal "tame" appeals procedure and Rio ultimately did the honourable thing, although I am sure that if he had gone to the civil courts on Human Rights issues he would have had a happier outcome. The courts could not have been seen to support such inequitable conduct by one of the quasi-organs of the state. I am sure that he was dissuaded from doing so by of the threat of Sepp Blatter to punish United if the matter went out of the footballing authorities' hands (the same Sepp Blatter who turned a blind eye to Italian punishments of players for actually consuming performance-enhancing drugs). The ordinary Manchester United supporters felt justifiably that they were caught up in a political maelstrom of which they had little comprehension and certainly no control and, which, in truth, had no place in the football world but only in the business world.

CHAPTER 10
THE GLAMOUR GAME

I began to travel this road with the firm belief that the uniqueness of Manchester United's rise to pre-eminence from relatively ordinary beginnings was the result of one particular phenomenon, the Munich air crash. In tracing through the club's history, I have begun to appreciate that this is only one of the reasons. Like many other clubs from the domestic matrix, United was in a position to profit from any sudden upsurge in interest in the beautiful game. A new optimism was abroad immediately after the Second World War. It hadn't escaped the attention of the ordinary man in the street that this was the second major conflict fought in Europe this century. Whether or not it was fought in a good cause, it was a relatively uncanny fact that wars always seemed to do far more lasting damage to the working classes than they did to the toffs, who went back to their lives more or less as if nothing had happened.

The working classes came back from the Second World War with a determination to have some of the good life for themselves. It was never going to be the same as the aristocracy would settle for but entertainment was one of the key ways in which a life of drudgery could be changed into something more meaningful. There was no greater embodiment of this than the joy of seeing a bunch of working class lads kick a casey round a park on a Saturday, particularly if they were doing it in the name of your town and in your colours. Football was ripe for take-off. It needed someone to light the blue touch-paper and then some club to cling on for the ride of its life. These two requirements were fulfilled by Manchester United. Firstly, the inspirational appointment of Sir Matt Busby (and Jimmy Murphy, his army colleague and first team coach) brought to the club from its City rivals a man of vision. His vision was of how football should be played and also how, up and down the country, there was a gene pool of boys of such phenomenal talent that, if they could be brought to one team, they could be world-beaters. The name "The Busby Babes" was first coined in writing by the

Manchester Evening Chronicle in 1953 after a particular performance by the 17 year old Duncan Edwards against Huddersfield.[86] That was the beginning of the legend.

The next station of the cross was the first time that team swept all before them in the League (1955-56) and their first entry into the European Cup (famously beating Anderlecht 10-0 in their first home match). Talk began then of their being the best in the world but they were to get a rude awakening of sorts from the team which would become the ever-recurring foe, Real Madrid, beaten 3-1 away and losing 2-0 at home before turning on the style to come back to 2-2. The 1950's version of the *galacticos* were then reduced to time-wasting in order to see themselves home and Bobby Charlton, who scored in that match, has ventured the opinion that if the match had gone ten more minutes United would have won 4-2 and taken the game into extra time. Big games were more free-scoring in those days!

The Cup Final of 1957 played its part in the legend too. The foul on United's goalkeeper, Ray Wood by Peter McParland of Aston Villa, was nothing less than an assault and battery. McParland came from ten yards back, when the goalkeeper had held the ball for two seconds and was moving out of his goal, to clatter him viciously in the face, shattering his cheekbone. McParland collapsed, cynically holding his head, an action which may have saved him from being sent off with one of the first televised examples of lenient refereeing. With no substitutes, let alone substitute goalkeepers, the double had gone for that year but many television viewers for the first time saw an injustice, which could only consolidate the romantic vision of Manchester United.[87]

---

86   See James Leighton's *Duncan Edwards The Greatest*. Jackie Blanchflower and Denis Viollet also played that day and Henry Cockburn (England's incumbent left half), Stan Pearson and Harry McShane were left out. It was the beginning of the changing of the guard and the precursor of the 1995-1996 season.
87   In an uncharacteristic show of temper, Edwards only just managed to restrain himself from assaulting McParland. Ironically, and by a freak of nature, the Irishman was one of the pallbearers at St. Francis's Dudley when his young opponent's body was brought home from Munich on 26th February 1958.

Duncan Edwards in full flight

With these heroic setbacks United was gathering a nationwide following second to none and the club was the talk of the football world when it embarked on its next attempt at the European Cup in the 1957-58 season. Its place booked in the semi-final that year (following the 3-3 draw in Belgrade), in which it would avoid Real Madrid and instead play A.C Milan, the stage was set to go at least one better than the previous year and at least reach the final. The experience of the two leg match the season previously and the knowledge that the team had finished that match the stronger meant that the prospects of actually bringing back to England the championship of Europe was very real. It had the football public, not just Manchester United supporters, in a frenzy of anticipation. The popular West Indian singer, Cy Grant, performed his version of the *Manchester United calypso*, the words of which are still sung from Old Trafford's terraces.[88] The team was seen as an embodiment of the gods. An ancient myth tells the story: the son of Odin was a demigod; common steel could not wound his body. He was beautiful and the best-loved of all the immortals. Once upon a time he dreamed a dream which seemed to forebode his death. The gods held a council and resolved to make him secure against every danger. The goddess Frigga took an oath from fire and water, metal, stones and earth, four-footed beasts, birds and creeping things that they would not harm him. He was deemed invulnerable so the gods amused themselves by setting him in their midst and shooting at him, hewing him with great swords and throwing stones at him. None could harm him. But Loki, the mischief-maker, was irritated by this and he learned from Frigga that she had taken no oath from the mistletoe because it had seemed "too young to swear". Loki plucked the mistletoe and gave it to the blind god, Hother, to shoot at the young god and "do him honour". Hother, innocently, did as he was bid and the twig pierced the young god through and through so that he fell down dead.

In the same way, the Football Association of England was irritated by Sir Matt Busby's preoccupation with Europe. Forgetting very quickly the dual lesson of the Magical Magyars in 1953 and 1954 respectively it was determined on its own xenophobic ways and United would have been in serious trouble if it had missed or sought to postpone the Saturday game against Wolverhampton Wanderers. The emphasis therefore was on getting home that Thursday at all costs. The cutting of the mistletoe fell to the well-meaning and totally innocent Captain Jim Thain. He took the decision to try another run after advice from the station engineer, William Black, that a re-tune of the engines would mean an overnight stop in Munich. Frank Taylor told Albert Scanlon, "Sod this! If you don't take off first time in the RAF, you scrap it." No one paid any heed

---

[88] Cy was a regular performer on Cliff Michelmore's *Tonight* programme, providing a synopsis of the news in calypso form at the end of the show. The Manchester United calypso was, however, written in 1955 by the Trinidadian artist Edric Connor.

and the flower of Manchester was doomed. The invulnerable young god was destroyed. The myth had now taken flight.

It could still have crash-landed just as severely as the Elizabethan in which those young men travelled to their deaths, however, if it had not been for the re-birth. After the initial shock of the crash had set in, the nation began to will on to success the survivors and those who previously had not been good enough to fill their boots. It was as if a wave of emotion could give them attributes, which had been somehow wanting in their physical prowess to that date. It saw them through to a Cup Final in which they were defeated by an ageing Bolton Wanderers side which, even on a bad day, would not have stood a prayer against the Babes, and another cruel defeat in goal-keeping controversy, albeit the charge by Nat Lofthouse on Harry Gregg was, at that time, within the rules of the game, given another lenient Cup Final referee who saw nothing wrong in it anyway. After that an ice age set in but United was already fixed in the public mind as something a little special in football terms. When it came back into the news with the capture of Denis Law from Torino in 1961 for a then British record fee of £115,000 the pundits began to nod their heads wisely. United was on the way back. It took time. The F.A Cup win against a Leicester team which finished second that year in the First Division, whilst United finished one place above the relegation places, began the comeback, just as it was to once again in 1990.

Whether, however, the team would have survived those dark days if it had not been for the emergence of George Best and the fulfilment of Sir Matt Busby's dream of lifting the European Cup, fittingly at Wembley in 1968, is a moot point. The dearth of success in those early years might have strained the loyalty of United's international band of fans, even though it would never have daunted the then largely local following who went weekly in numbers equal In a mainly standing room only stadium) to the more middle-class crowds of today, to Old Trafford. As it was the fairly-tale triumph at Wembley was Sir Matt's vindication, his way of saying sorry to those brave knights he had led abroad in an effort to make his club the greatest of all time, and who, as a result, had lost their lives. Fulfilling that dream was the last link in the chain of the legend. It was to prove strong enough to sustain the club through 26 lean years without a championship win. It was sufficient even to make the club more attractive than the successful clubs in those years. Again, just when the legend might appear to have become frayed at the edges, just when people might have begun to query, well, exactly who the f... are Manchester United, the Babes were reincarnated. Dream on.

George doing what he did Best

These are some of the reasons why, at the turn of the millennium, Manchester United was supreme among the football teams of the world, in a class of its own in effect. The club had, as an ethos, a profound belief in the development of the best young talent. It played football with a cavalier style and a spirit of Romance with a capital R in the sense that it is understood as a mediaeval concept. Its rise coincided with a new optimism in the life of the industrial north when, debilitated by two terrible wars and exploited in labour, the working classes found escape and vicarious self-fulfilment in the skill of the football player, the epitome of the working class hero. The tragic cutting of its first flower and the feeling that the authorities were somehow gratified by it led to a wave of emotion, which would have its backlash in later years. This carried the club forward on a tidal wave to the 60's and was not dissimilar from the "us against the world" mentality which Sir Alex Ferguson was to inculcate much later. It didn't matter then that we weren't winning; the group ethic between players and fans alike was more important than any match. Together we were strong.

The club's "second coming" then coincided with the Swinging Sixties, the days when British popular culture was the envy of the world, and the arrival, in George Best, of the first footballing pop star, a cult icon in his own right. The magical reverse of the tragedy of '58 was enough to endow Manchester United with almost superhuman qualities. Although the team did not prosper as well as it should through the 70's and 80's it still had enough good players and played football with sufficient panache for its followers to believe that good times were not far away. Its ability to beat the great sides of the time, memorably Liverpool in the Cup Final of 1977, which prevented the Merseysiders from annexing their own treble, and Everton in the Cup Final of 1985, despite having a man sent off with the score at 0-0, saved it from becoming an also-ran. Still, second was nowhere and greater things were expected.

United's third renaissance again coincided with a new movement in football. Just as it had in the 60's, football became sexy again in the 90's. Liverpool had great teams in the 70's and 80's, so did Brian Clough's Nottingham Forest, but no one could accuse Cloughie of being sexy and, sadly, Liverpool lacked its sex symbols too. John Barnes was about as close as it got. The sexiness wasn't, however, all about the male-female thing, although the culture of glamour created by George Best in the 60's was about to be totally eclipsed by a shy and retiring young man from Leytonstone.

Becks did not perhaps have the fifth Beatle's skill on the ball, although his are talents not to be undersold in the modern game, but he certainly had the image off it. With the assistance of a pop star wife and a battery of public relations people, he set about exploiting it in a manner which had not been seen before and is unlikely ever to

Or perhaps not. The fifth Beatle with Miss World

be repeated in quite the same way again. The two things, club and player, are, however symbiotic in the creation of this mythology. The club had to be right for the player's image to be right. David Beckham had to play for the most famous club on the planet for him to become the most glamorous footballer on the planet. Strangely, Eric Cantona, another who was equally glamorous but who shunned many of the trappings of glamour, had to go before like a John the Baptist to announce his coming. Oddly enough, David could never have achieved the same iconic status at Real Madrid. They had to buy the finished article. That is essentially the club's M.O. If their propaganda is to be believed they cashed in on David's image to the extent that, despite the fact that, with him as one of the mainstays of the team, the club won nothing other than *La Liga* in 2007, they sold enough shirts in his first season with the club to recoup the transfer fee. Florentino Perez went on record to say that Real Madrid would never sell David Beckham whilst he was President of the club.[89]

Just as its earlier reincarnations had caught and ridden the wave of a new mood in the social life of the country, Manchester United's renaissance in the 90's owed much to the same. Satellite television had changed the face of the media. A global audience beckoned for football. The sport was catching on all over the world, particularly in the Far East and the United States. English was the *lingua franca* and Britain was the founding home of football. The North West of England had some of the most famous clubs in the world. A global audience waited with bated breath for something phenomenal to come out of the old country and Manchester United did not disappoint. Flush with millions from the flotation, with a fan base growing exponentially all round the world and with the merchandising prospect that brought in its wake, Manchester United, a team which did not seem able to break out of its self-created rut, suddenly did something absolutely world-shattering: it acquired Eric Cantona and suddenly its fortunes were transformed. If ever the country needed a French knight, then once it was Lancelot but now it was Eric the Red.

Old Trafford had lacked a charismatic King for some time. Cantona himself had delusions of grandeur but did not really appreciate that he was a King. After all, he had been told many times by his many and various managers and by the French Football Association that he was nothing more than a jumped up frog. The King and his Kingdom found each other at exactly the right moment and, if the relationship

---

[89] He did indeed resign his first term in 2006 and was not reappointed until 2009. David left Madrid after the 2006-7 season.

was not to be all sweetness and light, it was exactly what the public in many countries wanted to see. The rest is most certainly history. Everything Cantona and United did was newsworthy, even when the haughty Frenchman didn't mean it to be. When he did such things as jump into the crowd at Crystal Palace in 1995 and knock seven bells out of a racist thug, the newspapers and the fans of other teams bayed in their jealousy that he should be kicked out of the game. The flip side of the coin was that Manchester United fans the world over loved him for it. Who did not wish that he had the courage to do that to such a despicable toad in full view of the world's press?

Cantona was larger than life and, if any reminder kick were needed, he made Manchester United realise it, too, was larger than life. If Eric had wanted to be a global superstar in the same mould as David Beckham, he could have been. He could have been absolutely

Eric Cantona - FA Cup (1996)

anything.[90] However, he had a serious side to him, one which hated

---

90   To a certain extent he is. He still trades successfully on his great reputation with

media trash and the pop culture. He needed to be understood and appreciated for who he was and for his immense talents, not merely for what he was perceived to be, and he craved a kind of academic respect. If anyone wants evidence of his influence on Manchester United, they simply have to attend a match at Old Trafford many year's after the Frenchman's departure, particularly in the heart of winter when something is needed to warm the cockles, and hear the refrain of "Five Cantonas" still echoing round the stadium, or towards the end of the season when holidaying is on everyone's mind. What encapsulates the carefree days more than the name Eric? So in the modern era, Manchester United, flush with money from the flotation, again caught the crest of the social and, in particular, the media wave and, just as Georgie had before him, Eric came down from heaven to convert the world to football, the Manchester United way. Just as the calypso goes: "football taught by Matt Busby." Just when he was most needed a torchbearer came to carry the flame. That he was then to become the catalyst for the fulfilment of the United prophecy was simply too much but Eric oversaw the reincarnation of the Babes and, with it, the emergence, in terms of popularity, of the greatest footballing "personality" the game has ever known. If anyone wants to ask whether an apparently underachieving Manchester United is really entitled to the sobriquet of the greatest football club ever, then perhaps it should first ask why David Beckham (and before him George Best) didn't emerge from Real Madrid or one of the other pretenders to the title? If John Carlin is right about Real Madrid's permanent pre-eminence in the game of football, why does the Spanish club serially fail to create its own teams?[91] It sounds like yet another ABU take. The fact is that Ferguson may have decided for purely footballing reasons that the Beckham entourage was no longer in the best interests of United and if another club wanted to take that on for purely commercial reasons then that simply defined where we were at.[92]

Manchester United 17 years after quitting the game.
91   *White Angels: Beckham, Real Madrid and the New Football* - September 2004. Carlin is also credited as the writer of the book about Nelson Mandela which spawned the film *Invictus*.
92   In 2007 Ferguson, talking to Nick Harris of the Independent put the blame firmly on his marriage to Victoria.

Becks and Teddy with the Grail (1999)

John Carlin is unlikely to answer because the truth isn't simply about football. It's about England, Englishness or Britishness, if that concept still has the same cachet as it once had, and something quite fundamental to this island race: the inheritance of the Romantic tradition. In a way strange in itself, because it is unlikely to have ever been in the distinctively Essex boy's mind, David Beckham was, at that point, redeemed. After returning in disgrace from his faux pas at the World Cup of 1998 when, on international duty, he contrived to get himself sent off for a stupid foul on Diego Simeone of Argentina and, in so doing, potentially cost his country a place in the quarter finals of that year's tournament, many thought he would be forced out of Manchester United and the English game by the vitriol pouring down from the terraces from the fans of opposing clubs.[93] In fact they jeered too soon. Instead he became, in the Champions League Final of 1999, the epitome of that chivalric vision of England and Britain. He could be Sir Galahad for a day. No matter his faults, he became, along with his team mates (because it is a team game and the table is round) the knights worthy of the Holy Grail.

---

[93] In London an effigy of this rather whimsical and unassuming Leytonstone boy was hanged outside a pub.

CHAPTER 11
SEVEN YEARS IN TRAFFORD

The great European cup teams of the 1970's and 80's were, in order, Ajax which won the trophy 3 times in succession between 1971 and 1973, Bayern Munich which achieved the same feat between 1974-76, and Liverpool which won it four times in 1977 and 1978, 1981 and 1984. The Liverpool triumph also marked a dominance of Europe by English football teams as Nottingham Forest (2) and Aston Villa won the trophy in the same period. Of the German clubs other than Bayern only Hamburg (1983) had won the trophy until Borussia Dortmund in 1997. The Dutch clubs have fared the same, both Feyenoord in 1970 and PSV Eindhoven in 1988 having lifted the cup. Five clubs from England (complemented most recently by Chelsea in 2012) have achieved the honour and that remains a record unmatched by clubs from Italy (AC Milan, Inter Milan and Juventus), Germany (Bayern, Hamburg and Dortmund), Holland (Ajax, Feyenoord and PSV), France (Marseille only), and Spain (Real Madrid who in 2014 won the *Decima* and Barcelona).

It is interesting to see how the three clubs which won the cup in the 70's and 80's have declined subsequently. Ajax was the first to repeat its triumph (1995). Bayern had to wait until 2001 (and 2013) and Liverpool until 2005. In all those cases, other than Bayern (which has featured in five finals in the period from the loss to Manchester United in 1999 and the last win in 2013), the solitary triumph was usually an oasis in a desert (although Liverpool again reached a final in 2007).

The "reign" of Alex Ferguson began inauspiciously and continued in that vein for longer than was comfortable but the barren period from 1986-1989 has to be seen in the context of what occurred after 1993. The rekindling of the Busby youth policy was probably not all down to Ferguson but he presided over the seed-sowing and ultimately he reaped the harvest with a generation of players (often referred to as "the class of 92") who became the cornerstone of the club's success for the next 20 years. He also had to break up an *ancien regime*, an aristocratically complacent team which had become accustomed to being a cup team, capable of beating the best on its day, and which may well have wanted the league title enough but was not prepared to put in the hard miles to earn it. Of that pre-Ferguson team and some of its great players only Robson and Hughes survived at United into the 90's (Hughes had to be brought back from Barcelona and a loan spell at Bayern Munich).

Robson's first league title in 1993[94], when he was well into the twilight of his career, was well deserved but something of a footnote to the career of a player who perhaps never did himself justice in the famous red shirt not because of his performances, many of which were simply world class, but because the great majority of his teammates were simply not from the same mould (there is a similarity with Steven Gerrard at Liverpool, for whom the moment has probably gone - i.e. he will probably never lift the league trophy although at least he has had the consolation of a Champions League win).[95]

The Cup Final of 1990 ended the Ferguson barren period but the Cup Winners Cup win of 1991 and the League Cup win of 1992 did nothing to alter the impression that United's was still essentially a cup team. Indeed the collapse in the league in 1992 was little short of catastrophic and it was followed by an inauspicious start to the 1992-1993 campaign. The stage was, however, set for the arrival of the catalyst to consistent league success and ultimately domination in the shape of Eric Cantona, who became eventually the general of a new breed of young cavaliers from the youth cup winning team of 1992. That team's leader, Giggs, was the first to flourish and the last to fade, In a sense he was one who was expected to and might have had the charisma to aspire to a similar sort of celebrity as Best and Beckham and whose talent was greater than the latter's and the equal of the former's in everything other perhaps than the purely selfish act of goal scoring but, ultimately, he was like his even more self-

[94] He played enough games in 1993-1994 in an unfamiliar number 12 shirt to get a second championship medal and he amy see the European Cup Winners Cup triumph of 1991 as his finest moment in a United shirt.
[95] Liverpool could improve on their 2013-2014 showing but the competition will be stiffer.

effacing and equally talented colleague, Paul Scholes, in that his only real interest was in the football, not in the fame.[96]

The colours are pretty firmly nailed to the mast as far as the greater question posed at the beginning of this book is concerned. Manchester United did steal a march on all its competitors in the half century between the end of the Second World War and the new millennium and the reasons why are plain to see and I will set them out in detail a little later but what of the original question? Was the 2005 FA Cup Final a kind of swansong for the club? Well, in the short term, the answer is certainly not but what about the longer perspective because there are many who will say the seeds of the 2013-2014 failure were sown back then or even before that Cup Final?

There is of course a limit to how far one can go back because one might as well say that the seeds of all genetic activity were sown as soon as the first descendant of amoeba crawled out of the swamp or maybe you would go back earlier to the Big Bang theory of the creation of the universe which holds that everything in existence, living or dead, was created in a microsecond at the ignition of this spontaneously combusted, explosive expansion.[97]

But I would prefer to start somewhere else. If I may at this point paraphrase the opening lines of Wordsworth's *Tintern Abbey* remembering these precise lines from the point where I stood in their memory when I stayed at the village en route to attending that memorable occasion (but all-too-forgettable match) in 2005, the one with which I opened this history:

Seven years have passed; seven summers, with the length of seven long winters!

---

[96] Finally retiring in 2014 after 23 years in the top flight. There were occasions even in that last season when he rolled back the years.

[97] The name was coined by Fred Hoyle in a BBC debate in 1949. He was in fact the theory's greatest detractor. Many dislike its almost vulgar connotations. Hoyle always claimed he meant it not to be derogatory but to be striking. See e.g Michio Kaku *Parallel Worlds*. It is factually inaccurate in the sense that the bang, if it occurred, was from something much smaller than an atom so it was not big, neither was it a bang as there is no air in outer space.

And in that time I have not shunned Old Trafford as have those who have joined the F.C United of Manchester experiment, or those members of the Manchester United Supporters Trust who called for a general boycott. I can report, too, that for me and for the great majority of the supporters in the stadium the period has been an enjoyable one:

in which the burden of the mystery
in which the heavy and the weary weight
of all this unintelligible world
is lightened.

But this really brings me round to the feeling which predominated that day and to the subject of this book. Let me make it clear that it started life as a requiem or at least as an epic lament for times which we felt had gone and might never come again. Wordsworth's poem was of course written about the enduring and eternal force of nature and its presence in all of us and in all the things which we manufacture with our minds and our bodies. So, just as he revisited the scene of a past existence, it is time for me to re-examine the record and see if the requiem was justified or if life springs eternal in the new shoots of the great red tree which to some may be a mere football club but to others among us is a creature beyond history, one which has passed into myth, and one which gives to its adherents a mystical and divine experience that can only be understood by those who have profound faith in the gods of men.

The truth told by the record is, of course, that the fears of those 2005 funeral attendees were not realised. United was eclipsed for a short time by the new kids on the block, Chelsea, but then came back with a bang not a whimper, won three titles in a row and the European Cup (or Champions League) for the third time, followed by a runners-up medal in the same tournament against the then imperious Barcelona at a point when United might have hoped to be its first winner twice in a row. A solitary Chelsea success in the Premier League was followed by another United win, another runners-up medal in the CL (again to Barcelona) and another Premier League even after the infusion of gold bullion into the poor neighbours Manchester City led to their getting a first league title on goal difference in 2011 - 2012.

The point of this is that, if you look at the record before the Glazer takeover of the club at the end of the 2005 season and then re-examine it again after the retirement of Sir Alex Ferguson in 2013, you will see the two records are pretty well comparable. The growth of the non-organically, super-rich clubs has introduced another dimension of competitiveness and United's team, under the inspired hand of the manager, has risen each time to the challenge. This competitiveness has been fuelled by the money which probably belonged in truth, in the case of Chelsea, to the Russian people and, in the case of Manchester City, to the people of the Gulf. The former, despite an apparent brief flowering of a democratic system, had no say in the oligarchs' acquisition of wealth in their unregulated society and the latter may not acquiesce willingly to their ruler's claim of right to the black gold beneath their shifting sands but they too have no real say in the matter because their social framework is not democratic. However, neither the British Government nor the Premier League has raised any concern about these arrogations of public wealth to private and capricious use, nor has either ever been much concerned at the commercialisation of the game by businessmen and that has of course been going on for generations. The reality of this is that predatory behaviour is tolerated even in civilised societies and if the predator is big and bad enough he or she will become a celebrity, even a hero to some.

The phenomenon has since been repeated in Spain with the ownership of Malaga and Mallorca and in France with Paris St. Germain and the sudden reappearance from obscurity of Monaco. In Italy it perhaps began with the Fiat family's ownership of Juventus but was given a nouveau-riche twist with Berlusconi's acquisition of A.C Milan. Until the latter became Prime Minister of Italy and perhaps perceived himself as having a somewhat broader church to satisfy, he certainly ensured that the original Milan club ruled with a cheque book. Only the Germans seem to have stayed aloof from this as the Bundesliga rules do not admit of foreign ownership but even if this seems to have led to another resurgence of German football recently (there have been many over the years and the German teams do not lie long in the doldrums) it is a dubious proposition for the league as a whole because it encourages the maintenance of the status quo. Thus, just as in Italy in the 80's, AC Milan overcame every team in their path and a sort of parity was only reconstituted when Berlusconi acquired his wider brief,[98] so in Germany there is really only one team, Bayern Munich, which prolongs itself often at the expense of its domestic rivals by buying their best players in a way which has gone out of vogue in England.[99]

Many Germans would argue with that analysis of course, particularly the big rivals in the north such as Borussia Dortmund, but it's fact. The German political approach to football is aimed at keeping Bayern Munich on top. Wealthy foreign ownership of another club such as Dortmund would threaten that hegemony. The German authorities are ultra-conservative in that sense and don't like interference with the status quo and the Bavarian club has a massive political lobbying machine aimed at keeping it that way.

The reality is that if the same political approach had applied in the UK, where successive governments of whatever hue have been far more wedded to the American laissez-faire model of capitalism than the German interventionist one, then there is no doubt we would have a German situation here, somewhat similar to the current Scottish model where, in the temporary absence of Glasgow Rangers from the top tier, there is only one team and that is the city rivals, Glasgow Celtic. If we had that German situation here it would benefit Manchester United more than any other team so it must be remembered that, in looking back over the post-Glazer record and making any fair and impartial criticism of it, we should be careful of what we wish for because the reality is that, in the English Premier League of twenty clubs, there is strong competition of varying but quite close quality between six teams, another four or so which are upwardly mobile and looking to get into those top positions and play

---

[98] Berlusconi's first term as PM of Italy was in 1994-1995 and coincided with AC Milan's initial decline. Despite his sullied reputation which has seen him convicted of tax fraud and sentenced to 4 years imprisonment (commuted to one year's community service in a care home!) and 7 years for statutory rape, he has been one of his country's longest serving prime ministers. He cannot be said to have left it any better than he found it.

[99] The predation in respect of Dortmund must be particularly hard to take for the northern German club's fans. Gotze, Lewandowski and now perhaps Reus and Hummels? There should be a law against it. Mergers and Monopolies perhaps?

lucrative European football regularly, and then ten or so clubs which will always create an equally strong if less intoxicating competition, in the terms of Pele's "Beautiful Game", for the three automatic relegation spots.

There is nowhere else in the first class game where you can say that and certainly not in Europe. In Spain there are regularly two competitive teams, Real Madrid and Barcelona[100], in Germany seldom more than two for any prolonged amount of time (of which one, Bayern, is always there but the other may change), in Italy two or sometimes three and in France the changes have been rung with the dominant club, Lyons, having fallen behind PSG because of the increased non-football investment into the latter club. The effect of this investment in England has been to promote two relative Cinderella / yo-yo clubs, Chelsea and Manchester City, into behemoths of the modern game. Indeed only perhaps Real Madrid can compete with these two in terms of the funds which the owner is prepared to put at their disposal to acquire players and "buy" trophies and Madrid does this largely, as Manchester United and Barcelona have traditionally, from football-related revenue. Many would argue with considerable justification that, in the case of Madrid, there is a government and city banker-led conspiracy to keep the club at the top, and this is to some extent to the detriment of Barcelona which, as a wealthy club in its own right, has always been seen as a symbol of the Catalan independence and resistance movement as much as it has as a sporting icon and representative of the nation of Spain. It is somewhat uncomfortably that it has had to be accepted and lauded as such by a Madrid government probably embarrassed by the club's recent footballing success, the impression its players have made on the Spanish national team and its consequent unparalleled success after many years of being a second-rate international side.

The Madrid government and the glitterati of its patrician society would no doubt have preferred that the capital's own teams, particularly the one with the prefix Real to its name, had contributed

---

100   I may be slightly cynical in treating the emergence of Athletico Madrid this season as temporary just as that of Valencia has proved to be in the past. Chelsea have already raided the club for its best players.

so richly to this exciting period of Spanish footballing history but of course Real Madrid has had to play the supporting role, providing, in the building of this metaphorical sporting cathedral, the journeymen drones for the highly skilled craftsmen of the Catalan club. How it must hurt!

Thus, refining this even further, only Real Madrid, as a symbol of Spain and the Spanish Government, has the financial clout to keep pace with Manchester City, Paris St. Germain and perhaps Monaco in the financial stakes. Chelsea has it to a slightly lesser degree (because its owner is just one man and his billions are not inexhaustible as are, apparently, those of Sheikh Mansour, unless the people of the Gulf decide that his generally enlightened despotism - although others would point to a horrendous human rights record - is no substitute for freedom of thought and the people's ownership of the country's natural assets). Bayern Munich also has it apparently, despite the absence of foreign ownership and despite the absence of support which often goes to a nation's capital's clubs, and despite having some of the fairest and cheapest match day ticket pricing in the world. Notwithstanding all these apparent disadvantages the current German champions have been rolling in sufficient money to lure to the club some of world's greatest football talents not to mention Europe's most successful manager of the last few years, Pep Guardiola.[101]

So, having already accepted that we don't want a situation where one club seems to have a monopoly on all the success a nation's football competitions have to offer, where have Manchester United ended up in all this under the Glazers? Well, the first point to note is that never since the Glazer takeover until 2014 and an apparent crisis has the club attracted a real overseas *galactico*-type talent and at no time did it show a desire to compete for those players. Cristiano Ronaldo doesn't count as, like Nani and Anderson, he was bought as potential and the club assisted in turning him into the *galactico* he is today. The greatest blossoming of his career has taken place in Spain where

---

[101] Albeit there are signs that, after the much-hyped publicity of 2013 about the German superpower in football eclipsing all opponents, this may not be the match made in heaven that some made of it. Certainly what it did to Barcelona in 2013 has been revisited upon it in 2014 by Real Madrid en route to its 10th European title.

he has eclipsed most records and has been driven to even greater efforts by the proximity of his great rival, Barcelona's Messi.

Cristiano Ronaldo with the Grail (2008)

When Arsenal (a team whose last trophy was that same ill-won and fortunate one which prompted the start of this book back in 2005[102] and which has underperformed more on the pitch and in the transfer market than any other since its decision to leave its Highbury home for pastures new at the Emirates) paid £40million, or thereabouts for Mezut Ozil from Real Madrid, where was United? Did they believe they already had that player in the more value-for-money Kagawa?[103] If so, why wasn't he having the same impact?[104] It is possible they did believe that because this has been the mantra of Alex Ferguson for many seasons - that there is no value in the market. No value

---

102   Until its 2014 cup final success against Hull.
103   Kagawa was sold back to Dortmund by Louis Van Gaal in 2014.
104   After an early good start Ozil's form has also faltered.

since the £32million acquisition of an equally under-utilised and ultimately dejected and rejected Berbatov? So little indeed that you can afford to isolate your overall best-performing player in Rooney to the extent that it was no secret that he wanted to leave the club and probably would have if Ferguson had remained in charge?[105]

The truth is that Ferguson acquired a reputation for being devious and secretive in his dealings - not only with the media but also with the club's own fans because of his constant trotting-out of the party line, which sounded very much like the Glazer propaganda machine speaking. Whether or not that is true we will probably never know although the propensity for "kiss and tell" memoirs suggests that we may learn something at some time in the future.[106] There can, thus, be no doubt that Ferguson's achievement of taking United back to the stop and staying there for seven years was magnificent, particular after the spending freeze imposed upon him by the Glazers. But it is hard to forget that it was constantly denied and lied about as if we should believe in a fairy tale - as if we should all see that the emperor in fact wore the finest possible apparel on his person and also could acquire more of the same whenever he wished from the designer player-wardrobes of the world. The one thing the fans will find very difficult to forgive the Glazers for is this imposition on the club of a culture of deceit and the fact that they embroiled one of its two greatest manager in that culture.

Yes, the club has done well under their governance; no they have not been interfering owners in the Abramovich mould; and, yes, they have been patient and given the manager time. They adopt a low profile; Fergie swore by them; David Gill swore by them; they have been comparatively good owners. But...

---

105   One of David Moyes's achievements was to make peace with Rooney, although not all United fans saw it that way.
106   The latest outpouring wasn't very informative on any of these matters. There was perhaps a little light on Jaap Stam and Roy Keane but it was very partisan. See Alex Ferguson: *My Autobiography*. It does have more than a hint about it of a memoir thrown together to catch the mood before the public memory fades or maybe even as getting the retaliation in first, which was very much a Fergie media-management tactic.

CHAPTER 12
SCORCHED EARTH

It is time to talk of the Glazers. This wealthy American family with an interest in a substantial sporting franchise in the United States[107] bought the club in a toxic deal which loaded it with debt, utilising a loop-hole in UK company law which allows a company with sufficient credibility with its creditors to acquire a target company without its being an assisted purchase - i.e. one acquired artificially by the reliance upon the target company's assets for the funding proposal. To an outsider or simply to someone exercising common-sense, this was an assisted purchase but there is a grey area where the law recognises no distinction between reality and the appearance of reality. As soon as the target has been acquired the transfer takes place to the target company of all the borrowing which the acquirer has raised in order to bankroll the deal. Thus the now wholly owned target company sees its assets mercilessly stripped out of it for the benefit of the new owners without a moment's hesitation, in fact with a hedonistic Thatcherite flourish. The process is all organised under several different companies sometime apparently under separate ownership although in fact having the same ultimate owner so there is always an appearance to that common-sense observer of the interaction of smoke and mirrors. The apparently illegal thing has been achieved by taking a legal route; the law has been circumvented: the letter of the law has been observed; the spirit of the law has not.

That is what happened with Manchester United. There was a half-hearted attempt to stop it by a similar group to that which had thwarted the proposed Sky acquisition back in the late 90's but it was caught on its heels by the speed of the Glazers' attack. To say it was aggressive is an understatement but it wasn't hostile as far as the

---

107   The Tampa Bay Buccaneers are an American Professional Football team based in Florida and is an expansion team – i.e one from a city with no history of professional football but which joined the NFL as part of the expansion of that league in the 1970's. It is the only expansion team to have won the Super Bowl. (2002). They have not contested a final since.

majority of the shareholders was concerned because, by this time, the overwhelming majority of the United equity had been concentrated in very few hands and, notably, one of the significant shareholders was the group of Irish racehorse owners and bookmakers, John Magnier and J.P. McManus, also known by the sobriquet of the *Coolmore Mafia* after the stables from which they raced their horses. Sir Alex Ferguson was himself to some extent the midwife of this sale because it was he who, in hail-fellow-well-met days, had persuaded his Irish racing friends to buy shares in United and it was a symbiotic relationship, too, because they gave him part-ownership of a seemingly good but (or so they thought) not necessarily brilliant racehorse called *Rock of Gibraltar*. This was in fact a significant conflict of interests and it is one which Manchester United as a Plc should not have allowed to occur.

The horse turned out to be a world-beater[108] and it was when the relationship between the owners and their manager deteriorated that the racing pigeons came home to roost. The Glazers pounced; the Coolmore group, which, in happier times, had been put forward as a prospective purchaser of the remainder of the shares, a sort of Fergie cartel, was only too glad to sell at what seemed then a generous price. The other major shareholders followed suit and there were insufficient ones in private hands to prevent a clean sweep.

The method by which the company had been floated left no discretion in the club or its directors to stave off non-footballing interest by the creation, for instance, of a golden share with additional voting rights or rights of veto, which would of course have considerably diluted the value of the shares if it had ever been brought into effect[109], and that is presumably why the precaution was not taken. When Manchester United was floated with Martin Edwards at the helm it was floated so that the board could cash in on its value. This meant that there was no defence to the Glazer strategy other than the belatedly mobilised IMUSA and MUST[110], which

---

108   The European Horse of the Year 2002 after 7 consecutive Group 1 wins.
109   That was always impossible given Martin Edwards' attempts at sales to Maxwell, Knighton and Murdoch. No way would he have contemplated a golden share which would have reduced his family's return.
110   Independent Manchester United Supporters Association and Manchester United Supporters

were swatted aside like flies and have been whining around in largely ineffectual manner ever since hoping for a day when they might be able to acquire enough United shares to make a difference. It is a forlorn hope although it is good that they are making the effort.

Whatever euphoria had greeted the staving off of the attempted Sky takeover was lost in the recrimination which followed the successful one of the obscure and very private, if not secretive, American family, which did not appear to have the best reputation for fair dealing - well not in its own homeland at least. A number of horror stories were told and the family was demonized. There were threats of serious repercussions involving violence and even death, so high were feelings running, but the Glazers ignored them all. They didn't bait anyone; they weren't in the fans' faces; they were models of good behaviour, staying diplomatically away from Old Trafford whilst the fans vented their fury in slogans and songs. Crucially, they backed the manager. Whether they saw him as a possible enemy, with his traditional, Glaswegian socialist leanings, is difficult to say but they certainly moved swiftly to appease him and, in making him the most important person at the club, they showed how advanced they were in their thinking. At the same time they demonstrated that the quickest way to Ferguson's heart was to pander to his ego.

So the upshot of the takeover, despite the anger of a significant number of the fans, was that, if it was not all good, it wasn't as bad as expected either - apart from the fact that the new owners turned the club into an opaque, propaganda machine and the money which might have been spent on improving the team was instead spent on paying down the debt they had incurred to buy it so that much that went through the turnstiles etc. was all dead money.

On the former point the club's website, like many in fairness in this new era of secrecy and opaqueness, is a model of disinformation as is the television network. If you wanted to know the truth about anything which was happening at the club, you certainly didn't expect to find it out from the club's official media. The various pundits would trot out a lot of what appeared to be lies except for the fact that they didn't know the truth either; they were totally in the dark too. In fairness it cannot be said that the club's official media were ever a source of reliable information about the team but post-Glazer they became a propaganda machine. That is how Manchester United now worked, how it still works. The truth, on anything of any moment, had no value because it might just reveal how precarious the club's finances were in this period. This giant of the football world, which at the beginning of the millennium, had been officially the richest club in the world, didn't actually have a pot to piss in unless the Glazers lent their takings back and it was just as well that the players, which Ferguson already had at the club before the new owners came, were of high quality and still had many years of success in them.

On the second point much has been said elsewhere in this book and will be repeated in more detail a little later of the sums which the Glazers have taken for themselves and their various creditors in order to bankroll the deal. Even a fraction of that poured into the squad would have sent United cantering over the hills and far away from its closest rivals. A counterweight to this profligacy, however, was Sir Alex's newly-discovered dexterity in the transfer market, particularly the shift of his focus into bringing in young players who proved also to be of the right quality. One can't help but think that necessity is the mother of invention. This magically acquired power[111] gave him, at least, the ability to overcome the immediate problems which this shortage of money had caused and which everyone, including him, was attempting to deny. It was, however, as many fans could see and be vociferous about, a mere papering over of some of the cracks. The bottom line is that Ferguson did not go after marquee signings because he couldn't compete – not simply with Real Madrid and Chelsea and later Manchester City, but also with many others who were not having to operate under such tight financial constraints. Whilst claiming that he was doing so because there was no value in the market he was in fact forced to shop in the bargain basement, except for the odd trophy player such as Berbatov,

---

111 He has had spectacular successes in the transfer market (e.g Hughes, Cantona, Stam, Solskjaer etc.) but spectacular failures too (Djemba-Djemba, Veron, Prunier, Bellion etc.) but the change of focus produced results.

for whom he broke the club's transfer record, because he would have been in desperate straits without at least one big signing. This may well have been the price he insisted on from the owners. The fact that the Berbatov transfer was protracted straight through to the end of the window shows the extent to which the purse-strings were being held by the owners but they were savvy enough to know both that you don't give in to another hard-nosed dealer like Daniel Levy and also that it was necessary once in a while to cast these pearls before the multitude.

If Robin Van Persie had been available a season earlier than 2012 - 2013 at a semblance of his true value, instead of the deflated value in his year before leaving Arsenal, he would have had to go to Manchester City or some other cash-rich club, not Manchester United. The shambles in the transfer window at the beginning of the 2013-2014 season simply demonstrates that the club could not compete for its main targets. It is common knowledge, for instance, that Ferguson was keen to sign Ozil when the German forward went to Madrid[112], but there is no way the club could in 2013 have matched the £42million which Arsenal eventually paid. And in some ways that may be good, because the football business seems sometimes to be totally out of kilter with what is happening in the rest of the world.

But it is not good if you are Manchester United and you are purporting to be the biggest club in the world. Even the acquisition of Fellaini was incompetently conducted in an attempt to get him at a cut price, which rebounded on the club in spectacular fashion.[113]

The fact is the hard core of United fans see themselves as having been conned. The board, the manager and all the pundits of the club's media have been complicit in this con, even though in the latter case they will probably have had less information than the external media because they will not have dared to ask the relevant questions. On the other hand the owners won't see this as a con.

---

112 See e.g Guardian 8th August 2010.
113 £22m would have triggered Fellaini's transfer but United let it lapse and ended up paying £27.5m - various but see e.g Mirror 5th Sept. 2013

They will see it as a bit of Realpolitik in a hard, financial world, one which went into near financial meltdown some three years after their acquisition, and that a degree of secrecy was necessary so as not to trigger a repeat of the desertions which led to the formation of the much-vaunted but scarcely flourishing FC United of Manchester, together with widespread panic and the negative effect on ticket sales.

The simple fact was that the machine Ferguson had created, with judicious and sometimes expensive recruits, was good enough to stay at the top even in a changing Premiership landscape. And the record certainly demonstrates that they were proved right by that. This is precisely what happened. The only question you can really ponder after such an era of success, which parallels largely what happened in the previous decade, is whether things could have been so much better and I am sure that the judgment of posterity will be that they could have been; that what was achieved would equally have been achieved even under the ponderous and cumbersome Plc with its stock market regulations - in other words Gill and Ferguson, a pretty formidable executive team in any industry, would have found a way to make it work, and so much more would have been achieved anyway because the necessity to reward shareholders would not have taken the same toll on the club's finances as the obligation to repay the creditors artificially created by the Glazers and their debt-financed acquisition.

The only question to be weighed in the balance is whether the economies and efficiencies introduced by the new owners, which were so essential to their repayment plans, and their own entrepreneurial zeal and ability, gave an adequate counterweight to these depredations so that one more or less replaced the other. The short answer to that is that, in time, it might prove to be true. There is no doubt that they are spectacularly better businessmen than anyone at the helm whilst the Plc was in charge and I have no doubt that the best witness to this would be Gill. But the corollary to that is that it isn't true yet. It isn't true in the period we are talking about and it is to some extent academic because now the captain of the ship, Sir Alex Ferguson, is gone and so is the golden generation of players who manned it, it is the immediate future from now on which will show which side of the fence the club has fallen.[114]

The club spent £71m in the financial year 2012-2013 merely financing the cost of the debt[115], equivalent to the transfer kitty of even the largest European teams. Of even greater importance is that, since the takeover, United has spent £680m in financing the purchase of itself, a sum more or less equivalent to the stated cost price[116]. This was simply absorbed by the club's vast revenues but it is dead money because it is going solely to pay for its own ownership. Manchester United is possibly not the only good ship mug enough to reward buccaneers for boarding her - that is probably par for the course for piracy - but it is certainly what has occurred.

In this regard, if you are looking for the reasons for the initial success and the fact that it was sustained during that period of cash-control, which still effectively exists, despite considerable in-roads having been made into the debt, you can't just say it was the manager, of fundamental importance though he was with his ability to reinvent himself at least twice (firstly with the appearance of Arsene Wenger in 1996 and then with the appearance of Jose Mourinho in 2004). To get the full picture you really have go back to that nucleus of great players who delivered successive championships. It is well recognised that there were three great teams in that period but certain players stand out. You can single out from the first phase between 1990 and 1995 Schmeichel, Cantona, Kanchelskis and Hughes. After that Giggs and Scholes have been the ever-presents ably assisted by Beckham, Keane, Butt and Cole during the decade or so after that first team and since then of course world-class players like Rooney, Van Nistelroy, Berbatov and Ronaldo continued the development until 2009 or so.

---

114   Louis Van Gaal's immediate achievement on taking over in 2014 was to make the owners wake up and smell the coffee. They shelled out a reputed £165million on new players and this might not have been necessary with a better and earlier recruitment policy.
115   Guardian Sept. 18th 2013
116   This was US$1.5bn or £790m at the prevailing exchange rate.

Rooney at the European Cup Final (2008)

Since the departure of Ronaldo, however, there has been a dearth of that same world-class quality, only partially alleviated by the recruitment of Robin Van Persie from old rivals Arsenal. The team has aged with its manager but there is considerable uncertainty as to whether the younger generation can replicate the success of the last one and this is the point at which the marquee signings become relevant. This is the time United needs the injection of one or two really exceptional players to help the established stars and to nurture the undoubted talent which is coming through. Even in this regard the rules have changed so substantially that identifying young talent at an early stage is no guarantee of its staying with you when it comes of age as a number of recent examples have shown[117] because it not only the clubs which have become more savvy, the players have too or rather their agents have. For a multitude of reasons this is the crunch moment for the owners. What they do now will demonstrate whether their claim of May 13th 2005 to be "long-term sports investors and avid Manchester United fans" has any ring of truth at all[118].

Most fans, even those with the reddest of the rose-coloured spectacles, know that these signings are needed to provide the extra

---

117   Gerard Pique and Paul Pogba stand out as examples.
118   Daily Mail Online 11th April 2006

spark for the team and the jury is currently out, not on whether they are there – the propaganda suggests that there is doubt as to whether they are but it is propaganda because the club has never really tested the market, they've just talked about it. There is no doubt, for instance, that, if the propaganda were true, United could have bid for players like Sergio Aguero, Ya-Ya Toure, both of whom went to City, Eden Hazard, Juan Mata[119], Oscar, all three of whom went to Chelsea and, perhaps the most obvious one, Mezut Ozil, who went to Arsenal but it is no secret that, before his transfer to Real Madrid, he was the one player whom Ferguson actually coveted for his midfield and with good reason because he is the mercurial type of player who can do a job similar to that of Paul Scholes.[120]
It's fine of course if United didn't want any or all of these players but is it possible to believe that? What are they if not world-class? That is not the point though. The question is whether United has the attractiveness, the will and the means to go toe-to-toe with the traditional big clubs and the nouveau-riche arrivistes[121] to bring these players to the red half of Manchester. I say the jury is out but the answer might be seen to be an emphatic no. It's not going to happen. United will invest in potential but not in established quality. The progress will, therefore, continue to be hit-and-miss, except for the odd marquee buy.[122]

Either way, it is what it is. The question now is where does it go from here? Assuming that the fans are generally in the mood to forgive the wholesale rape of the clubs' assets in order to enrich an opportunistic, sports-entrepreneurial, North American family leveraging them to over twice of their previous net worth, what can they expect from the owners in the future? Have we in fact missed the opportunity of painting a picture of domestic and European hegemony in the quarter century or so we have just gone through which might have been similar to that of Real Madrid in the 1950's

---

119   Although of course Mata was bought in the January 2014 transfer window at a handsome profit for Chelsea. It was a popular buy but a panic one.

120   There is a suggestion that he was offered to United but at the time the price was too steep. After a good start he fell out of favour at Arsenal. He may have fared better at United.

121   One cannot underestimate in this equation the attraction of London. Once you could say if you want the night life, go to London; if you want to play football, go to United. It is not quite so true now.

122   LVG has made significant in-roads into this policy.

and early 60's and Liverpool in the late 70's and early 80's? I rather suspect again that in the real world that is precisely what we have done. We did have the opportunity; we did have the wealth; we did have two exceptional opponents in Real Madrid at the beginning of the decade and Barcelona at the end and we accepted second place too easily to those opponents.

It is probably time, therefore, to analyse in greater depth the period from the Glazer takeover, which was launched finally on April 14th 2005 (although it had been pre-empted by some preliminary skirmishing such as the removal of three directors from the United board some six months previously) and was completed a mere two months later on June 14th with the family's announcement that it had acquired 97.3 per cent of the Plc shares. This took the majority owner past the threshold (95%) needed to get rid even of any dissentient minority. It was that easy; it was that much of a walkover. Despite all the talk about scorched earth, making the club toxic for generations to come, despite the board's apparent reluctance to endorse the bid, the manager's emphasising his non-capitalist roots, despite a number of questions asked in the mother of parliaments by politicians of the left aware that the club was in in fact a community asset (and not one just of Greater Manchester but of the more diffuse global community), and despite the opposition of a number of fans, celebrity and common man alike, Malcolm Glazer, by mid-June, would have been justified in repeating the *vidi, veni, vici* of a previous conqueror. Whether the phrase is rightly attributed to Caesar's British campaign or to some other victory of the last century before the coming of Christ[123], Glazer was the new Caesar of the Premier League and, incidentally, a lot of his countrymen would follow him[124].

The first thing to look at is the ownership at the time the corporate raid occurred and at the opposition and what it was doing. The previous October the club had terminated discussions with the

---

123 Cf Plutarch *Life of Caesar* and Suetonius *Lives of The Twelve Caesars*.
124 Stan Kroenke at Arsenal; John Henry and Tom Werner at Liverpool; Randy Lerner at Aston Villa; Shahid Khan at Fulham; Ellis Short at Sunderland. None of these guys are football fans; they all have their eyes on the money.

family and the board was aggrieved by the tit-for-tat removal of three of its long-established directors. In February 2005 Gill was still describing the revised proposals as "aggressive" and "potentially damaging" to the club's long-term prospects but by the following May everything was much more cosy. It is easy to see this in simple terms as a result of the Glazer tactic to reassure the management team that its position was safe one day after after acquiring the Coolmore 28.7% but is it so simply explained in such Quisling terms or was there indeed a total volte-face of officials who had suddenly seen the Glazer and the corporate business ethos light? Why, in short, was this famous institution allowed to go so gentle into that American night?[125]

Well, a bit of it certainly has to do with that old story of a man and a horse.

---

125   Apologies of course to Dylan Thomas.

CHAPTER 13
ROCK OF GIBRALTAR

How could a racehorse actually bring down an institution? The short answer may be that it can't but it certainly looked back then as if it might. Why the Coolmore owner, John Magnier, made Ferguson a present of part-ownership of the stallion (with the Irishman's wife Susan as joint owner) is unknown and perhaps the horse wasn't expected to achieve what it did in its two years of racing at the turn of the millennium. It looked like a lucky break for Fergie but you do have to be careful of what you wish for. Just as the real Rock has been a constant cause of controversy between the United Kingdom and Spain, particularly since its importance as a strategic naval base has declined with the similar decline of the British navy and of the likelihood of war between exhausted European states, so proved the racehorse. It was named after the island; its mother bore the name *Offshore Boom* and it was felt fitting for Gibraltar's post-war status as a tax haven for fleeing British capital to be recognised in the horse's name. Maybe Magnier and McManus kept much of their wealth in this offshore haven. Either way, a bit like the real thing, the horse only become a problem after it had been retired from active service.

Whatever the rights and wrongs of the Magnier - McManus / Ferguson deal, Sir Alex did not show the same generosity in giving back what had apparently been given to him quite freely (although I acknowledge that this is merely a one-sided reading of what occurred and may not be the whole truth). Some years after the creature retired from racing and was earning "real money" from the serendipitous life of siring offspring, he threatened to take his main shareholders to court. The crisis was headed off ultimately by a deal which saw Sir Alex accept a one-off payment of £2.5m to relinquish his interest in the horse[126] but if he felt that was the end of the matter

---

126   At least one writer Martin Hannan has criticised this as a bad decision on the basis that an offer from Magnier to share in the stud fees for a period would have netted Ferguson that sum per year but perhaps by then he was tired of it or he did not trust the Coolmore clan to deliver if he remained

he was very sadly mistaken.

There is no provable reason to believe that the decision by the Irish racehorse trainers to sell out to their co-investors, the Glazers, in June 2005, was motivated by anything more than profit but John Magnier would not have been human if he had not enjoyed his moment of Schadenfreude. He was very much standing on the bridge and although it wouldn't be right to say it was Ferguson's body he saw floating by beneath him, that moment cannot have been a comfortable one for the club's manager. He had already had to endure the campaign of vilification (the 99 questions to the board of Manchester United) and traditionally his relationship with the board hadn't been that great. He had of course famously announced his retirement in 2001, to take place at the end of the 2001-2002 season.[127] It is possible that the dispute with Coolmore would already have been looming and might well have been on his mind to the extent that he could be thinking he could do without the hassle. Indeed, it has been suggested that, after yet another set-to with the board about his contract, he threatened to retire in the 1998-1999 season, the one which in fact ensured his legacy. There is something in this. Brian Kidd left in the same season to take over the poisoned chalice of the Blackburn Rovers post and there were suggestions then that Fergie was not looking after him properly, at least in the monetary sense. Certainly their relationship does not appear to have survived that spat, if such it was.

But the truth is probably that Sir Alex had enough on his plate looking after himself.[128] It is impossible to say if he was already disenchanted with the owners at that point but certainly they would exact their vengeance when they jumped ship in 2005, at the point when United and the Ferguson / Gill axis in particular wanted the shareholding to stand firm against the American onslaught. It is noticeable that, as late as 2011, Sir Alex's former skipper, Roy

---

involved.

127   BBC News 18th May 2002.
128   In *Managing My Life* Ferguson refers to the fact that Martin Edwards and Peter Kenyon felt that every time a manager's job came up they had to offer Brian a new contract. Without saying it outright Ferguson implies that Kidd was less than transparent in his dealings with the club at this crucial time (immediately before the December 1998 last group match with Bayern Munich).

Keane, the man whose exploits were the most praised by his manager for his unselfishness in the way he saw his team through to the Champions League Final in the memorable match with Juventus in Turin in April 1999, was critical of his old boss, following the exit from the Champions League in a group match against Basle, accusing him of putting his own interests before those of the club and citing the saga of the racehorse as evidence[129] of the fact that the manager was prone to do what was best for himself rather than what was best for the club. Keane has of course become something of an isolated figure since his acrimonious departure in 2005 from United in the aftermath of criticism of his fellow players after another of the relatively rare Champions League exits (this time against Benfica) but it must have hurt even a man with a rhinoceros skin for a wound of that nature to have been reopened from such a surprising source.

The racehorse is probably the principal reason why the club fell into American hands. When the dispute about *Rock of Gibraltar* broke out in 2003, Magnier and McManus were already the largest United shareholders and, as part of their overall strategy to win the war, attempted to have Ferguson removed as manager. The board responded by trying to bring alternative investment into the club at a time, coincidentally, when Avram Glazer was looking at investment into European football as a means of diversifying the sports interests of the Glazer family in the United States. He took up the United general offer in March 2003 without there being anything to suggest that it was anything more than a. a modest investment of approximately £9m for a 2.7% stake. However, in September 2003, shortly after the new season had begun, the investment was increased to a level where it had to come on to the board's radar and by November it was 15%. The family stayed, however, below the 30% at which an automatic bid for the whole is triggered according to public corporation takeover rules[130]. It was not until 12th May 2005 that the Glazer family reached an accommodation with Magnier and McManus to acquire their 28.7% interest which then effectively took their holding to 57% and triggered automatically the

---

129   Interview Sunday Times December 2011
130   The UK Takeover Code – when a person or a group acquires 30% of the voting rights of a quoted company they must make an offer to the other shareholders of at least the highest price paid in the 12 months before the offer was announced.

takeover offer.

The "poison pill" is a tactical device often used in company takeovers to defeat a potential hostile takeover by creating a shareholders-rights plan in which the existing shareholders have the right to buy shares at a discount if an external shareholder buys a certain percentage of a company's shares. That way the predator can't negotiate with the company's shareholders individually but only with the board. In this case the tactic was reversed. External shareholders were invited to acquire shares to prevent the majority shareholder from exercising powers which might be damaging to the company's (the club's) overall interests but no one gave any thought to what might happen if those shareholders then got together and by-passed the board. There was probably not the slightest inkling that it might happen until the dispute between Ferguson and Magnier / McManus threatened to go to court. The Glazers may well not have welcomed this; they may have wanted to sit on their investment without ever having to go to the massive expense of making an offer for the remainder of the shareholding, but their hand was forced by the potential damage to the share price, which protracted court proceedings would most certainly have brought about.

Thus, Ferguson, without doubt the saviour of Manchester United in one sense, was also the potential architect of its downfall in another: a real example of a fall from grace, a prodigal son story in reverse. But it didn't happen that way because, under the Glazers and under the newly-galvanised Ferguson, United did not fall apart as the prophets of doom had suggested. Ferguson had been disillusioned enough in 2001, shortly after winning his second series of three titles in a row, a feat not achieved before and still unrepeated by any other club in the English first division, to feel compelled to announce his retirement with one year's notice. Simultaneously he announced his intention to have nothing further to do with the club, no ambassador role, no directorship, no nothing. It sounded as if it had all ended in tears but that same Ferguson suddenly found himself with a new lease of life and probably the best owners he had ever experienced, certainly in his career at Manchester United. Where he had apparently[131] been undervalued up until then by a board mainly composed of blimps like Sir Roy Gardner, who was still maintaining that he had been right about the toxic nature of the Glazer takeover as late as 2010, calling it an unsustainable model, about which he was of course wrong, he was suddenly the most important person at the club.

What a PR coup by the new owners! The old school management had neglected the club's greatest asset; the new boys dusted him off and gave him pride of place. And if the new business model was expensive (for the club and for the fans) it was certainly not unsustainable and it led to arguably the single greatest period of Manchester United success on the field. Indeed the club had, only two seasons before Gardner's sour grapes pronouncement, wrested the Champions League trophy from difficult opponents for the third time (this time from Abramovich's Chelsea) and had gone back to the final in 2009 only to lose to a great Barcelona side (as they would again in 2011).

The truth was that Ferguson understood the Glazers. Like him they were winners and they were in charge. He had no time for committees and Plc boards and warring factions of shareholders. He was a great believer in "the boss is the boss, the manager is the manager and his job is to manage, the manager is the most important person at the club". It is a maxim of Hermetic Philosophy: *as above, so below*[132]. Whatever happens on one level of reality (physical, emotional or mental) happens throughout all levels. It is possible to understand the universe through the self and, of course, power and control are things which Ferguson understands only too well. I doubt if there is a recorded instance of his ever having a falling out with the Glazers, precisely because he knew it was an argument he couldn't win, nor to some extent would he want to because he trusted their savviness. The relationship was symbiotic. It was clear also that with them he couldn't appeal to any emotional attachment to the club. They might have claimed to be avid fans before they bought

---

[131]   Interview with the Guardian April 2010.

[132]   The Emerald Tablet of Hermes Trismegistus. The importance to life generally of this observation is difficult to exaggerate.

their first shares in early 2003 but no one believed that for a moment. Everyone knew this was a money thing. They would not have been so hated if they had stumped up the money from their own resources to buy the club but they would have been resented anyway because Manchester United wasn't an investment: it was an institution and a community asset.[133]

Ferguson was probably one of the first (along with an initially sceptical David Gill) to realise that the new owners, these powerful money-men from America, might just talk his kind of language and could, to echo Roy Keane's accusation of self-interest, be very good for him. In fact the Glazers were exceptional performers in the market economy of the United States, as adept as you could get without the slices of luck which accompanied Abramovich's amassing of a fortune or the somewhat dubious birth "right" of a member of the Abu Dhabi royal family. They were mighty beasts in that jungle, a regulated economy where entrepreneurs had to play by the rules of an elite of which people like them were not initially a part, the type which a strong man like Ferguson might admire. Indeed, despite not being terribly prepossessing or photogenic and despite not courting publicity or the public eye at all, the Glazer family was worthy of the mythical compliment that *here there are dragons*.[134]

Whether one loves or hates the Glazers one cannot but recognise that they have been phenomenal performers in financial terms. They played a blinder with the United acquisition, taking out the opposition in one of the most tactically adept hostile takeovers the City of London has ever seen. It was Blitzkrieg of the economic kind. Although it was known from the beginning that the cost of the acquisition would be something like £60m per annum in interest payments alone they never wavered in their belief that they could make it work and the simple truth, no matter how much organisations like MUST might deny it, is they did. Who they made

---

[133] Part 5 of Chapter 3 of the Localism Act 2011 requires local authorities to keep a register of community assets. Old Trafford was declared one in July 2013, a rare victory for MUST which nonetheless should not be underestimated.

[134] Inscription on the Hunt-Lenox Globe (1503 – 1507) relating to eastern Asia and perhaps a reference to Komodo.

it work for is another question and whether it would have worked better if they had never entered the arena in the first place is yet another, but work it did and they themselves, their energy, their ability and their know-how, were the main reasons for this. Whatever they have cost United, they have earned a large part of themselves, either by savings they have made in the previously profligate Plc spending prior to the takeover when, it seems, there were a few noses in the trough, or in the commercial *nous* they have brought to the business. The latter has resulted in some of the largest sponsorship deals in football history and in this department they punch well above even their significant weight.[135]

They have also been extremely loyal to their management team, not only keeping the promise made to Gill and Ferguson in 2005 but eventually appointing as Gill's successor, when he finally decided of his own volition more or less simultaneously with Ferguson, that it was time to step down, the ex-J.P. Morgan banker, Edward Woodward, whose main qualification was that he was in the Americans' acquisition team. He was in fact the banker who engineered their triumphant takeover in the first place. He got his reward, in the way these conflicts of interest always seem to occur either by accident or design in the banking industry, when he joined the club in 2005 as a financial consultant. Then he was promoted to be its commercial director in 2007. In that time and immediately following it he has paid his employers back handsomely and has overseen the increase of the club's annual revenue from £49m in 2005 to £118m in 2012. In that sense, if not perhaps yet in the football club management sense, he was the natural successor to Gill and this seems to be part of the strength of the Glazers: they know when it's not broke not to fix it and they have a way of finding round pegs to fit into round holes. This is why, in any analysis of them as a pernicious influence over the affairs of Manchester United, a cancer in an otherwise and preternaturally healthy body, there has to be added to the balance, perhaps grudgingly so far as many fans are concerned, egged on by ginger groups with agendas of their own, the counterweight of the benign.

---

[135]   £47m with Chevrolet and the huge £750m with Adidas in 2014 alone.

The cancer is of course what the media like to write of in scaremongering terms as "the debt" and it is time for a brief word as to its history. The cost of the club in 2005 was US$1.47bn and the Glazer family took on debt in their various corporate enterprises in order to acquire Manchester United Plc. This took the company into private ownership until in 2012, in order to reduce the debt load, the family went forum shopping for the issue of an IPO in a market which would be attracted to the shares, initially choosing Singapore (over Hong Kong) but finally settling for the safety of the New York Stock Exchange. The family's acquisition was of course completed back in the halcyon days before the fall of Bear Stearns and then Lehmans banks precipitated a near global collapse of the financial markets and I have no doubt that, despite the performance of the team in the interim, the Glazers will have felt the pinch from at least 2007 onwards, if not earlier. The reason for this was the way the acquisition was structured.

In the UK at the time section 151 of the Companies Act 1985 forbade the provision of financial assistance by a company to a buyer of its own shares. This might seem axiomatic but it is more complex than it sounds. The Act didn't define "financial assistance" but section 152 provided some examples of what would amount to prohibited activity. In broad terms the spirit of the statute meant that the Glazers couldn't rely on any assets of Manchester United Plc or any subsidiary company as security for the loans it intended to raise in order to buy the Plc and its subsidiaries. It had to be able to raise this money via its own assets and that can't have been easy because the Glazers weren't then *that* rich, the price was high and the takeover was initially resisted. Another twist to the takeover regulations was that they couldn't get the companies on the cheap: they had to offer for the whole shareholding at the highest price paid in the previous 12 months and that will have been more or less the price they paid to up their stake to the trigger amount of 30% of the issued equity. The Glazers were wealthy but in 2003 they didn't make the Florida rich list of those worth at least $US1bn.

So this was no easy acquisition and how do you raise $US1.5bn with less than $US1bn yourself? Well the trick is the loophole in the legislation. If, by hook or by crook and by promising the earth to bankers who see risk as octane fuel for junkies even on a bad day and who spend their spare time high-rolling at the poker tables of the world, you can raise enough money outside the target vehicle to complete the deal, then, once you have acquired it and taken it back into private ownership, it becomes your plaything and you can do exactly as you wish with it. In particular you can mortgage it up to the hilt. And that is exactly what the Glazers did: they leveraged the club to meet those blank cheques they had apparently so cavalierly written. But of course it wasn't cavalier at all; the risk was very carefully calculated.

From those comparatively humble beginnings before 2005 and in the period since, with a fortune estimated at $US4.5bn[136], the family has shot to number 2 in those same Florida rankings.[137] The main reason for this is that in August 2012 Manchester United became a Plc again when it floated on the NYSE and in March 2013 the club was valued at $US2.8bn, almost double the price at which it had been acquired. The family's other assets had grown also, if not quite so exponentially, so by then even the Tampa Bay Buccaneers American Football franchise was worth $US1bn. The family coffers were further enriched within the first three years after the purchase by unexplained payments of about £23m from the club.[138] Each of Malcolm Glazer's six children also borrowed £1.66m from the club in that period. The bankers and professionals who helped this happen, one of whom is now the club's CEO, took another £15m in the process. As one journalist put it, "Manchester United, formerly the proud, rich behemoth of the Premier League, [is] laden with the extraordinary debts of a takeover which nobody wanted, except for seven members of a family in Florida and their very well paid advisers".[139]

Ironically, after all the forum shopping described above, mainly in

---

[136] Forbes September 2013.

[137] Tampa Bay Times March 6th 2013. If one is looking for controversial billionaires, spot number 1 is taken by Micky Arison whose Carnival Cruise Line owns the good ship *Costa Concordia* which ran aground off the coast of Italy in 2012 with great loss of life.

[138] Published accounts of Red Football Limited, the SPV used to acquire the company, January 2010.

[139] David Conn: The Guardian 11th January 2010.

the Far East, they went back home for one very simple reason: the choice of the NYSE was dictated by the passage of the Jobs Act which President Obama intended, following the recession, to use as the catalyst to persuade smaller companies to float in the United States. It was something of an irony that the jobs which would be created were all in the UK but that's capitalism. If there is an opportunity, why not use it? The Plc became a Plc again and, although the initial start to life in the new market was sluggish, it has to be admitted that, since then, the performance of the shares has been very good. However, if the fans were to think for one moment, as flotation is a well-trodden exit route, that this listing heralded the ever-anticipated Glazer withdrawal from ownership of the club, that hope was quickly dashed in the short term and looks increasingly forlorn for the future too. At the initial public offering (IPO) the Glazers were offering to sell only A shares. They retained B shares for themselves and these contain ten times the voting rights of the A shares, which are an investment, not an invitation to a say in the club's affairs. A crucial paragraph in the offer document makes it clear also that the club will continue to be owned by the "linear descendants" of Malcolm Glazer, the five sons and one daughter who have already paid themselves handsome stipends out of the club's resources.

The purpose of this analysis is not to be a critique of capitalism. In October 2013, at the point of writing these words, the world was facing a financial crisis of gargantuan proportions because the Republican-backed US Congress was holding the US President to ransom over the fact that he wanted to provide health care to the poor. The provision of welfare to the poor has always been a hot topic in the States and who knows which side of the argument is right? That isn't the point, neither is it the point that the club was respectably acquired, without breaking any rules. By contrast the owner of Chelsea, Roman Abramovich, has allegedly been involved in Russian gangland killings[140], bribery of public officials, theft of the assets of others (companies and individuals) and his life seems to be one long law suit.[141] But he is wealthy to the tune of US$14.6bn[142],

---

140   The so-called aluminium wars. The killings ceased when Abramovich reached the top of the tree – c.f Times On Line 5th July 2008.

dwarfing even the Glazers' recent performance, and he is feted in London and no doubt has a special arrangement with the UK Government which forgives him the taxes paid by the ordinary folk who just happened to be born here. In recent litigation against his old friend, colleague and subsequent nemesis, Boris Berezovsky, he was described by an eminent High Court Judge as "a truthful and on the whole reliable witness"[143]. No wonder he is the darling of those ageing villains who used to head up the notorious Chelsea Headhunters gang, long time but little respected foes of United's own hooligan firm, the Red Army[144].

Sheikh Mansour, who owns Manchester City, is of course a different kettle of fish and off the scale in terms of wealth[145]. Nothing similar can be aimed against him and his reputation is impeccable. He was born with the proverbial silver spoon in his mouth but that is neither unusual nor the stuff of just criticism. Why he acquired Manchester City is unknown but it was certainly equivalent to a lottery win for the club. It might have been Everton; it might even have been Newcastle. Rumours abounded at the time as to his intentions in respect of one of those clubs and the factor which tipped him towards City may well have been his personal friendship with the previous owner, Thaksin Shinawatra, who had to sell his shares in a hurry.[146] The Sheikh's hand may have been forced. Certainly he was forced to write off City's £305m debt.

Hailing from a tribe of the Bani Yas Bedouin, which migrated to the island of Abu Dhabi over 200 years ago, he was a scion of a people which subsisted on the pearl trade until the discovery of oil in the

---

141   The Times 5th July 2008.
142   Forbes 2012.
143   BBC and Press Association (various) 31st August 2012. Ironically, the Judge, Lady Elizabeth Gloster (now of the Court of Appeal) was, as a Queen's Counsel, for many years the oil companies' advocate of choice.
144   See Tony O'Neill's account in *Red Army General* of Steve Hickmott's claim that the headhunters once "took" the Stretford End "with the appliance of Chelsea science". I haven't heard that Hicky took him up on his offer.
145   Estimated with a personal fortune of £17bn and family wealth of US$1trn.
146   Overthrown as Prime Minister in the coup of 2006, he acquired City in 2007 for a reputed £80m selling it a year later for £200m. (Bloomberg). Although initially giving him the post of honorary President of the club with no official responsibilities the current owner, proving to be fair-weather friends, did a U turn and dispensed with his services after his conviction for graft.

1930s. Trade was already well established with the British and had been since the 19th century when the area was known as the Trucial Coast (because of the truces with Britain to protect the trade route to India)[147]. In 1936 the partly British-owned Iraq Petroleum Company signed a concession agreement with the then ruler (the Sheikh's grandfather) to prospect for oil. The rest is history.

In the Middle East there is no true democracy and the land and its mineral wealth does not belong to the people. The Emirates style of government might be best described as enlightened despotism, similar to that which prevailed in Europe in the 18th century[148] and which is a more benign way of separating the haves and have-nots than those adopted by say a Saddam Hussein or a Stalin. All governments are built on this, even democracies, but in the latter advancement by merit is more likely, even if the few always have advantages over the many and, indeed, see the many as there to further the hegemony of the few. It should be added, however, that enlightened despotism was Plato's preferred style of government so it has a viable provenance.[149]

The downside and the hypocrisy in this is that the city states of the Emirates are in fact built on the efforts of lowly-paid migrant workers from India, Pakistan, the Philippines and so on, just as the ancient city states of Greece were largely erected by forced labour. Sheikh Mansour was a lucky guy because the bottom line is nothing more than that his great grand-daddy did a Jed Clampett.[150] For some obscure reason, and it may be because he has the prescience to appreciate that the Arab Spring will eventually lead to questions in his own house and he wishes to diversify as much as he can in the meantime to ensure there is more than one plate spinning in the air if gravity fails and things begin to fall about his ears, he wanted to

---

[147] It had previously been known as the Pirate Coast.
[148] Frederick 11 of Prussia, Catherine 11 of all the Russias and Maria Theresa of Austria-Hungary to name but three all practised religious toleration and brought about sweeping economic and administrative reforms without undermining the social order or weakening their own power bases. This is really what is taking place in the Emirates.
[149] See *The Republic*. There are echoes of this in the City States of the Italian Renaissance also.
[150] *Beverley Hillbillies* - a television show of the 60's in which Jed was the head of a dirt-farming family which struck oil and moved to Beverley Hills.

make the Bitters happy too. But I suspect that will be a harder task than any he has taken on previously. The City club's finances are shrouded in secrecy as one might expect for such a character. He may be the Deputy Prime Minister of his country, even at such a young age, but one suspects the qualification is a familial one and, in any event, the Sheikh does not embrace transparency.

For instance the financial injection which allowed Manchester City to defeat the UEFA financial regulations in 2010 came from Etihad Airways, which on the face of it seems perfectly acceptable and not at all an exercise in circumvention of accountancy rules. Except for the fact that the company which owns the airline is incapable of providing the money from its own resources because it has never declared a profit. Even so the myth continues: *"Etihad's 10 year, £340m deal to sponsor City's shirt, stadium and academy is about to enter its third year... they are a major commercial partner because they are effectively helping to underwrite the club."*[151] The truth is they are underwriting nothing because they are underwritten themselves. The real underwriters are the people of Abu Dhabi. The gap between Bin Nayan and Abramovich isn't ultimately a chasm. They both believed in their right to use someone else's money to get what they wanted.

The Financial Fair Play rules (FFP) are intended to be the antidote to this in the sense that they are aimed at preventing clubs from posting losses to achieve success and the reliance on a benefactor to fund club losses. They are seen by the nouveau-riche as an attempt by the establishment to preserve the status quo and that debate will lead to justifications for the kind of accountancy alchemy needed to sidestep the rules, as is already being practised for instance by PSG. A weather-eye was being kept on whether this would lead to any form of condign punishment in April 2014 or whether it would prove a damp squib. It certainly received censure.[152]

There is some force in the argument. Margaret Thatcher would have

---

151   Daily Mail 19th May 2013.
152   City were fined £49m and their CL squad was reduced. A mere bagatelle to the Sheikh but punishment nonetheless.

allowed natural forces to take their course and, if need be, exact their toll and which side of that debate you are on is probably determined by whether you are an interventionist or a free marketeer by nature. However, in purely football terms, as UEFA is European, the model is likely to be the interventionist German one rather than the American *laissez-faire* version which is periodically in vogue in the UK. Whichever it is, the likelihood is that it will be capitalist.

In a sense this is merely the reverse of the argument referred to above about enlightened despotism, which is merely another means by which the rich hang on to power, and results in part from the fear of democratisation, particularly that of the middle classes. That process is something which has probably always been a part of even primitively civilised society but the pace of it has quickened since approximately the 15th century. In England, although that concept of nationhood was relatively embryonic at the time, it began with the accession (some would say usurpation) of Henry V1 by Edward 1V in 1461 and the subsequent advancement of the new queen's family, who were seen as upstarts, although this criticism is not in fact entirely fair.[153]

Europe as a whole was somewhat later in its development but the principle of middle-class democratic hegemony is now well-entrenched there[154] and even the Emirates will find that the tide of progress cannot be halted. There is not as much to be feared from the poor as there is from the educated but perceptibly disenfranchised middle classes, as even the Russian revolution has shown at least temporarily and with some hope yet for the future. Indeed the Chinese revolution was led by the educated middle classes, the workers being utilized, as with all wars, class or otherwise, as cannon fodder. The Emirates have a relatively high living standard because of the mineral wealth but, as has been demonstrated elsewhere, this can be a recipe for disaster as the human condition is generally to take the yard when the inch is offered.

---

153   The then Queen Elizabeth's mother, the Duchess Jacquetta, could trace her ancestry back to King John without having to jump through the hoops invented by Edward to prove he was of Arthurian descent!

154   Nazi Germany proved that it is, however, more tenuous in Europe, just as, since, has the way in which the Russian people have simply ceded their hard-won democracy back to Vladimir Putin.

The point is not to make comparisons or claim any moral high ground for the red half of Manchester, although it will obviously and fairly be seen that way. There is discussion elsewhere in this book about the relatively serendipitous way in which Manchester United made its fortune (and lost it, some might say) and there can be no argument with all forms of evolution, just as there is no argument with the fact that the essence of the capitalist system is that there are winners and losers and that the one is the natural corollary of the other. The point is, quite simply, that in this context Manchester United is unique, not for any patriotic reasons and not even just because it is probably the best known football club in the world and certainly one of a handful of great clubs, all of which have been mentioned in these pages.

It is unique because it is the only one of these which carries this burden of debt quite so publicly. As demonstrated already it is not of course the only club which is in debt. Neither Chelsea nor Manchester City survive on their own resources. Each of them is dependent on a sugar-daddy type figure who could take his toys home any day if he so chose or if his personal circumstances were to change (as did those of the owners of Malaga and Mallorca). PSG and Monaco are in the same boat and paddling very hard for a perhaps mythical landing. Real Madrid is dependent on an internecine web of finance which would make for a convoluted conspiracy theory in itself and no doubt a Dan Brown type figure will write about it sooner or later. Barcelona is heavily in debt also. However, I doubt if even the Catalan giant, the most successful *team* of the past decade and arguably the best ever, could do what United just did and survive.

It is surely nothing to be proud of that United is unique in not only having been and remaining self-supporting but in actually having amassed sufficient inherent value to pay a poorer owner to acquire it. There is something fundamentally wrong about that, something which offends the sensibilities of right thinking people everywhere. Or is there? Is that just me and my rose-coloured spectacles? Of course there may perhaps be something special about this one but there is actually nothing unusual about the concept of the reverse takeover. It doesn't happen all the time but neither is it a rare bird of exotic plumage. When it does happen it is usually for easily discerned reasons: for instance, if the smaller bird acquiring the larger one is more energetic, more enterprising, more adaptable, growing as the larger one declines, it is explicable. But that wasn't the case here. These two weren't even birds of a feather.

CHAPTER 14
THE BANNER BRIGHT[155]

The team's dip, therefore, didn't coincide with the Glazer takeover. It was already there and it was triggered probably by Ferguson's first statement of his intention to retire at the end of the 2002 season. I have already speculated that things might not have been going well at that stage with the Coolmore shareholders, although little is known precisely of why he made the decision. It came after a period of unprecedented success – the treble followed by two more Premier leagues making United the fourth club to win a set of three titles in a row[156] – and he insisted that he was cutting his ties with the club. There was to be no directorship, no ambassador's role.

It was a strange statement and there is no doubt it hid an agenda of some sort. There had clearly been some rift with the directors which Ferguson had expected to see sorted out but no one was saying much.[157] It was all the odder for the fact that it came at a time when the purse strings were about to be loosened in spectacular style. United had acquired some big players in their time but very rarely had they paid record money and, at that point, Dwight Yorke at £12m in 1999 was the club's most expensive signing. Just before him they had paid £10.7m to PSV Eindhoven for Jaap Stam.

Then the figures began to sky-rocket. Ruud Van Nistelroy joined for £19m on 23rd April 2001 and Juan Sebastian Veron signed for £28.1m on 12th July 2001. United had been lining up the Dutchman's signature for some time and Veron's came out of the blue (the reports were that the club was interested in his Lazio team-mate Nedved) but in May 2001 things had got so bad that Ferguson felt forced to state that he was severing all ties with the club. The

---

155   The banner bright, the symbol plain,   Of human right and human gain   Then raise the scarlet standard high,   Within its shade we'll live and die,   Though cowards flinch and traitors sneer,   We'll keep the red flag flying here.
156   A feat they were to be the first and so far only club to repeat between 2007-2009.
157   The Times 19th May 2009.

decision is often blamed for United's falling behind Arsenal in the 2001-2002 season but a better reason might be the thoroughly flummoxing decision to sell Jaap Stam to Lazio, albeit for £16m, and replace him with the once great but visibly ageing Laurent Blanc. The speed with which this transaction was rushed through was bewildering. Stam insists he was told to go by Ferguson at a petrol station where he was filling up his car and was basically given no choice. He also stated that he was told that United needed the money from his sale.[158]

In fairness in a recent interview on MUTV (19th October 2013) Ferguson made the rare admission of a mistake in selling the Dutchman. But perhaps his statement that he had admitted this many times before didn't entirely ring true and perhaps also his suggestion that it was all about getting money in for the club was truer than the throwaway manner in which it was said might suggest. He *was* under that pressure. And perhaps also there were a number of conflicting motives. Once Ferguson falls out with you the sentence is death. It is pronounced immediately, albeit not always publicly, but its execution may be suspended. The latest superstar to understand that is probably Wayne Rooney, although we may never know the truth of whether Ferguson was carrying out his final vendetta, because Moyes took over and prevented possibly another admission of a mistake.

Stam did have the last laugh, to the chagrin of us all, in helping AC Milan dump United out of the Champions League in March 2005. The fact that Liverpool (somehow) beat the winners in the final in Istanbul to claim their fifth European Cup (from a fourth place finish in the Premier League the previous season) must have rubbed salt in the wound. Indeed many critics were saying after this defeat that Ferguson had allowed the standards of the team to slide since his then solitary triumph in 1999. This was one of the biggest criticisms against United: they did not kick on in Europe after that win. They had the opportunities: 2002 against Bayer Leverkusen, when the final would be held in Glasgow; 2003 against Madrid, when the final would be held at Old Trafford (these were two finals which

---

[158] Mail 11th November 2012.

Ferguson desperately wanted to get to); 2004 Porto and 2005 AC Milan. The openings were there but the team came up short.[159]

The double whammy of losing this rock of a defender and the uncertainty over the manager's future seemed to unhinge the team but perhaps a lot of things were changing. His relationship with David Beckham, the next to feel the other side of the double-edged sword of success, was certainly deteriorating and he admitted for the first time after his retirement in 2013[160] that he felt the player's marriage to Victoria Adams, whom he didn't even name but simply referred to her as "that Spice Girl" had made him lose focus. No one would have guessed the day that the two Spice Girls "Posh" and "Sporty" came to do the half-time draw at Old Trafford in November 1996 that they were witnessing the beginning of one of the most famous marriages of the 21st century or that the young man who had broken into the team so recently would go on to become the most famous footballer on the planet. Certainly no one would have guessed that the Manchester United-mad kid would be forced out of the door by Ferguson in 2003 against his will and for a relative pittance. That pittance would be recovered in shirt sales practically before the ink was dry on the contract because he was transferred to Real Madrid. And this was when United had, after all, just got their mojo back after losing the Premier League title in 2002, although they had been narrowly beaten over two legs by that same Real Madrid with its fabulous foursome of Zidane, Figo, Raul and the Brazilian Ronaldo, perhaps the only team of that decade which could have given the later Messi-Xavi-Iniesta-inspired Barcelona a game. The fact was that, at the end of the last millennium, that sort of domination was United's to lose, and lose it they did. On Ferguson's watch and long before the Glazers started to flex their muscles.

Thus, it is fair to say that United were already in a trough when the Glazers took over so they were not the reason for this apparent malaise. United duly got their trophy back from Arsenal in 2003 but were well beaten the following season by a team which had become so fond of itself, despite its flat-track bully failings, to begin to revel

159   See e.g Daniel Taylor's article in The Guardian 9th March 2005.
160   Interview with UBS October 2013.

in its hyped up media promotion as the Invincibles because of the feat of going through a season unbeaten (but without any record-garnering of points). Jose Mourinho then arrived at Chelsea and trumped the Arsenal's [by this time] self-promotion with one of his own as the Special One, although his reputation was very significantly fashioned on the failing of an assistant referee in the Champions League Quarter Final against United at Old Trafford when the perfectly good but disallowed Paul Scholes goal sent Mourinho charging down the Old Trafford touchline to celebrate the Porto goal that sent them through to the semi-final of a very soft European Cup. Without that win against AS Monaco, would the Portuguese strategist have got the Chelsea job and gone on to the heights he has conquered since? Perhaps. It is difficult to know how things would have turned out but certainly that triumph and United's scalp on the journey made a significant difference to his CV. He was also inheriting a team built by Claudio Ranieri to which he had to make very few additions (but those he did make were significant ones in Drogba and Essien).

Both United and Arsenal suddenly looked passé and this Chelsea team did prove powerful enough, fuelled by the Abramovich billions, to beat all-comers. They were technically excellent but built on power, just like Arsene Wenger's original teams, which could dwarf United's on the field, but not for heart and skill. Chelsea seemed to have taken the Wenger model and improved it to the extent that they still hold the points record for a Premiership season[161] and they racked those up in a number of games without apparently breaking sweat.

The next season wasn't quite so one-sided but the momentum was still with the Blues and they retained their title, the only team other than United to do this since the new format of the English Premier League began in 1993. There was no doubt that this was a shock to the United system and, because it coincided with the advent of the Glazers, it was always likely to be the case that they would be blamed.

---

161   95. Season 2004 - 2005

The protests began immediately of course but didn't really affect the traffic through the turnstiles. There were still fans stepping over the dead bodies to get in, even if every instance of the failure to sell all tickets for some of the matches was greeted with glee and prophesies of the doom and gloom which never quite materialised. The campaign had legs, though, even if they were scarcely the most athletic legs; the green and gold campaign, a continuation of the earlier venom, was still able to begin as late as 2010 but it was probably over as a significant protest by March of that year, when David Beckham, turning out in the colours of AC Milan on his peripatetic journey round the world (in particular to keep his international career alive), famously donned the scarf, the colours of the Lancashire and North East Railway-workers club, at the end of another Manchester United v AC Milan Champions League game, this time one which United won 4 – 0.

It was an iconic moment and one Beckham could make because he was long gone when the Glazers took over and he must have known that his chances of ever getting back to the club he had loved from boyhood were slim to non-existent, at least whilst Ferguson and those who doted on his every whim were in charge.

The campaign and Beckham's apparent endorsement of it didn't stop United selling out their season ticket allocation the next summer and it didn't stop the fans turning up at the 75,000 seater stadium in their droves. It isn't really surprising because, under the new ownership, United had gone on to win the 2008 Champions League final in Moscow, against the upstarts, Chelsea, to make it even sweeter, if that were possible,[162] and had also gone all the way to the final in 2009, failing to retain the trophy only because of the excellence of Lionel Messi and his Barcelona team-mates.

---

162   It is. The sight of John Terry distraught after missing his penalty in the shoot out and ultimately costing Chelsea the game is perhaps the sweetest moment of all.

Cristiano celebrates his goal at the Champions league Final (2008)

And that really is probably the key to the complaint: United were good but they were not quite good enough and the disappearance of £700m plus from the coffers could not be overlooked entirely in that criticism, particularly as owners like Roman Abramovich had already made it clear that he would not treat his cash injection into Chelsea as loan account. The fact that he couldn't, because the balance sheet would not stand it, was irrelevant to those fans dressed in the green and gold. The fact was that, if United had been owned by equity rather than by debt, the great team might have been good enough to beat even the best, which was epitomised then by Barca.

So this is basically what we had after the Glazer takeover: a great team in the world pantheon of teams but one not able, despite all the propaganda, to compete with Real Madrid, Chelsea and Manchester City in the European transfer market and, at the same time, United has been surpassed by Barcelona and Bayern Munich, if not in finances, then in qualities of attraction. If the money isn't there, the other attractions are insufficient. That doesn't apply to the Spanish and German champions and currently two of the best teams in Europe. That gap cannot be bridged unless the Glazers cease to take these vast sums of money out of the club. That is fact. Whilst they continue in charge and whilst they continue to behave in financial terms as they were then, United will always have to work harder than those other named clubs to stay at that top table. Under Sir Alex Ferguson they found a way. The question is whether that will continue with his successors.[163]

Finishing third or fourth and getting into the Champions League Group Stages every year may have been good enough for Arsenal, whilst it was going through its stadium rebuilding phase, Or indeed at Liverpool, where financial constraints have held the club consistently below the best except for that one rare and fortuitous triumph in 2005, but it will never be good enough to manage the expectations at Manchester United, which have resulted from Ferguson's management and his astonishing ability to reinvent both himself and his team, first of all after the French invasion of Arsene Wenger and then the new wave of attack under Jose Mourinho at Chelsea. Nor is it likely to be an option in the new age of the bottomless pits: not only Chelsea but an unfettered Arsenal and, of course, Manchester City and its Croesus of an owner, not to mention Real Madrid and the excellence of Barcelona and Bayern Munich.

---

163   United's recent expenditure demonstrates a welcome volte-face but can it be sustained under the present ownership?

It would be wrong, therefore, to blame the Glazers for the dip United suffered in 2004 – 2006. This was a matter of chickens coming home to roost from earlier neglect when the club had certainly not been short of money in the transfer market as and when needed. Conversely they have to be congratulated for their light touch management in the years afterwards and giving Ferguson the time to re-build. There is no doubt that, after his initial hostility to this capitalist takeover, which might have offended his Labour sympathies,[164] Ferguson got a new lease of life from the change of ownership. His mantra has always been that the most important person in a football club is the manager and there may have been a few occasions where the Plc board did not necessarily agree with him. Famously he is alleged to have been on the verge of quitting in 1999 and of course it was certain that he was in 2001. It was a breath of fresh air to find that the Glazers agreed totally with his philosophy and self-regard and that they had such faith in him. Nor would it be fair say that this was opportunistic on their part. One thing they appear to have understood, whatever the purists might think of it as a priority, is Manchester United as a business and they saw far better than any of the previous incumbents of their role that Ferguson was crucial to the operation of that business. And they were rewarded for that faith, because as soon as he had re-engineered the red machine, it blew the opposition away, just as it had previously.

What they cannot escape from however is the criticism that, despite the level of expectation, this was still not the domination which clubs like Real Madrid, Liverpool, AC Milan, Bayern Munich and Ajax had been used to in their respective heydays and which Barcelona, not Manchester United, was about to embark upon. Even Ferguson admits this to be a failing[165] and there is no covering up the fact that the club was deficient in experienced quality players in both its finals with Barcelona. The outcome might not have been different because that Barcelona team has been dubbed the best ever[166], although this is a little like the recurring elections of the greatest club player ever. Whichever way one turns this it can be argued that

---

164   The Independent 22nd September 2004

165   Interview with MUTV 19th October 2013

166   See e.g Graeme Souness Liverpool FC Official Website 27th May 2011

United did not give themselves the chance because they did not improve sufficiently after their 2008 success, even though, in the run-in to that European victory, they beat Barcelona in the semi-final and are likely to have seen from those matches how the Barcelona tiki-taka style was developing to a point where it would shortly become irresistible.

There is no doubt that Ferguson, with his own superstars, Scholes and Giggs, ageing, will have noticed that and will have wanted to develop it but the truth is that United were simply not in the running for the kind of player who would bring those attributes to the club. Much was made of the pursuit of the much vaunted Dutchman, Wesley Sneider, from his club Inter Milan, which did, in a reversion under Mourinho to Italian *catanaccio* tactics of a previous era, stifle the flare of an even more rampant Barcelona in their semi-final in 2010, but you will not find any but those who wear the most rose-tinted spectacles who believe that United was ever seriously in that race. It fell through because of money, and that, in all honesty, is where it has always fallen through, except in very rare instances of investment in those years in the marquee signing (Berbatov and Van Persie come to mind but both of these were established British rather than world stars at that point) rather than youth.

That marquee midfielder has been needed since 2008 and has always failed to materialise. One is forced to conclude that this is because the money was not there to afford him, even following the sale of Cristiano Ronaldo in 2009. Many questions have been asked subsequently about the utilisation of the £80m fee following that sale and they have always been answered by Ferguson, as the face of the club, that "there is no value in the market"[167] but it is odd how that problem suddenly surfaced after the disposal of Ronaldo, whereas it had not been in evidence before except perhaps in the failure to consider any marquee signing from a foreign league.

---

167   Quoted on Republik of Mancunia website on 12th August 2010 and repeated many times since.

CHAPTER 15
LE ROI EST MORT
VIVE LE ROI

Denis Law - The first king of Old Trafford

The suggestion also, in defence of the youth recruitment policy that the club is committed to bringing young players through, is simply not borne out by the evidence. Since the class of 1992 there have been no young superstars coming through the ranks. Wesley Brown, John O'Shea (both now plying their trade at Sunderland), Darren Fletcher, Jonny Evans are the only ones who have made their mark in that time, although Danny Welbeck and Tom Cleverley came through later.[168] All these have been squad players with the possible

---

168 Danny was sold to Arsenal in 2014 and Tom would also have been sold but elected to go to Villa on loan.

exception of the under-rated but physically susceptible Fletcher. The hyped talents on whom great praise has been heaped such as Ravel Morrison and Paul Pogba have, for different reasons, had to go elsewhere to find first team football. Now a lot of expectation is placed on the head of Adnan Januzaj and latterly on James Wilson. The record is not as great as Ferguson would have us believe. His strength over those years has been in bringing through mercurial young talents from other clubs but if you remove Rooney and Ronaldo (and latterly Rafael) from the list that is not the success story it would seem to be either.[169]

The second criticism which the Glazers cannot escape is over the amount of money which they have removed from the United coffers in their nine year ownership. This is now just about the equivalent of the sum actually needed to acquire the club in 2005 but a substantial portion of the debt is still there[170] and the simple fact is that it still takes some servicing, particularly if, in the same period, all the Glazer family are going to treat the club as one of their personal piggy-banks for the dubiously onerous duty of a seat on the board.

The club became the first football club to be valued at US$3bn in January 2013[171] but such valuations are speculative, as anyone caught in the 2008 credit crunch will tell you, and they simply cannot be relied upon. A better indicator is the potential acquisitions market. Who is going to buy a football club with that sort of value, even as a long-term investment in which they are seeking to recover their capital in say ten years when it took eight to reach the point at which the capital invested at the US$1.5bn purchase price has just in theory been earned (but has not been used to pay down the debt in its entirety)? It's an Alice-in-Wonderland sum, or, of more relevance to the state of origin, a Mickey Mouse number.

If it is correct, and it is a question on which the jury is out, it would be an unforgivable sin of Alex Ferguson if he has quite deliberately

---

169   In truth the youth policy has changed to one which does not engender the sort of club loyalty shown by the class of 92.

170   Sky News recorded this on 18th September 2013 as having fallen to £389.2m following record revenues of £362m in the 12 months to June 2013 from the partial flotation on the NYSE.

171   Forbes 27th January 2013

assisted the owners to con the fans. He is very much in the owners' corner and has been their apologist on many occasions when the fans would not have taken the same nonsense from anyone else at the club (and many of course have not found it acceptable even from him). It is an Emperor's New Clothes of a con. They are asking us to see things which defy logic and Ferguson is so often their spokesman. He may say that he is not a businessman and he does not involve himself in matters such as this but he is a political animal; he always has been. He knows black from white. It is a horrifying thought that he has joined the opposing camp, so horrifying that some will not even entertain it as a possibility. It is exactly his presence however which has reassured them by giving the club the feel-good factor to go with some of the marvellous results he has conjured out of nowhere. He has quite literally at times made bricks out of straw and even if that denigrates to an exaggerated extent a good and competitive squad no one should think that there is not an iota of truth in it. The cracks were there for all to see and the paper was becoming thinner.

There is no doubt that the manager's personal stock and his wealth have improved under the new owners and he was certainly worth that. If the previous regime did not treat him equally fairly then shame on them but this doesn't excuse the way he has covered for the Glazers and has been part of the propaganda conspiracy at United that the money to buy players was always there and was always available. It has taken a crisis of Moyes proportions to unearth any of it. He has exacted his price from time to time with the odd marquee signing such as Berbatov and Van Persie but these are all too rare. A team like United needs at least one of those each season to stay at the top. Instead, too often he has been forced to invest in unfulfilled talent or to shop in the bargain basement. Some might say, for instance, that this is precisely where he bought Van Persie and that, if the Arsenal player's price had not been so reduced by the fact that he was determined to leave on a Bosman at the end of last season if not allowed to go at the beginning, then we would not have bid for him at all and he would be a City player now. The margins are that fine. Where would the United of the 2012 - 2013 season have been without RVP? You got part of your answer in the 2013 - 2014 season. Rooney does tend to stand up when the others are missing but so often Rooney is the last man standing who makes us decent, not the one, like Ronnie or RVP, who makes us the champions.

In fairness perhaps to Ferguson he may have seen himself as the best man to manage United through a situation which he knew would otherwise be dire and his love for the club was so strong that he chose to make the sacrifice. If so there had to be an element of playing the game, pretending to kow-tow to the owners, but if that were true one would expect to see him on his retirement cutting all ties with the club and then coming clean, telling it like it is, telling us how he prevented our worst fears from becoming all too present reality. Instead we get more of what we have come to expect from the club's strait-jacketed media. Even under the Plc, MUTV and the related media were never a forum for free speech and, although I doubt United is much different from any other club in its censorship policy of anything which might adversely affect the operation of the club or cast any criticism on to its owners, one can still hope for the odd flash of insight, the odd crack in the wall. The censorship is, after all, pretty shameless and it is demeaning half of the time to the old stalwart players who make up part of the presentation team and it is an insult to the fans to see some of these famous players of the past trying to pretend that all is rosy in the garden when it is obvious to all the real fans on the outside that the exact opposite is the truth.

The natural corollary of this is that the same fans have always known that the good times simply cannot continue to roll unless the Glazers get real and start to pour the money back into the club's playing staff.[172] Whatever Ferguson's shortcomings as a human being (and I am sure his are no shorter than anyone else's) the reality is that he has been a wizard in keeping the club at the top, against all the odds, between 2009 and 2013, when the quality of his playing staff has been declining perceptibly year on year, except for the odd addition such as Robin Van Persie and the seemingly and mysteriously interrupted progress of players like Shinji Kagawa. The probability is that it might have needed another wizard to continue that work-in-progress,

---

[172] The welcome reinvestment this year as I continue to write this can't disguise the fact that a more regular budget would have obviated the need for such surgery, which is not even yet complete.

someone like Arsene Wenger, who so shook up English football with his arrival at Arsenal and who has worked with loyalty and composure through a lean period to keep his club competing at a high level with less spectacular results than Ferguson but miraculous ones nonetheless, or a Jose Mourinho who might have seen himself as a shoe-in for the job,[173] although it is difficult to imagine how his combative nature would have worked in fusion with the current owners.

The simple fact is that the gravy train simply could not continue to rattle along the track without some significant changes in the approach of the owners, who no longer have the comfort blanket of Ferguson's magic coat of many colours and his rabbit-producing headgear. It was too big an ask of any new manager, let alone one who had no track record of major success even at Premiership level. Indeed the job, in these circumstances, may prove to be the kind of poisoned chalice which the United job became after the retirement of Sir Matt Busby or the Liverpool one after the retirement of Kenny Dalglish. One wonders whether David Moyes will thank Sir Alex for his choice of chosen successor now that his very short interregnum has come to an end. We will only know when the dust finally settles and everyone has had their say but it is fact that he never got the chance to succeed. My fear for him was always that, without a total loosening of the purse strings, which would mean that the shareholders would be the ones to go short, any amount of time would have been in vain anyway. In fairness the loosening came but it was too little, too late.

Despite the six year contract it was always a moot point whether Moyes' job was secure against all financial storms and we learned at the point of his dismissal that it depended on a top four finish and qualification for the Champions League. At the time of his appointment I suspected that the minimum expectation was a top three finish. No one can guarantee the Premiership, although Ferguson could usually guarantee it twice in every three years at least, let alone the Champions League, which looks distinctly out of

---

173   So suggests Diego Torres in his book *Prepare to Lose: The Mourinho Era*. The club may now have that wizard in LVG but this perhaps postpones the problem for three years.

the range of this team despite their close shaves in the past five years, but what if there were a fourth place finish twice on the trot or what if, as actually happened, the unthinkable were to happen and there was no fourth place finish even? How long does the patience extend then? Moyes probably did not help himself by jettisoning Sir Alex's tried and trusted back-room staff to bring in his own relative "rookies" but he may have proved resilient to pressure in that as the evidence suggests that Sir Alex recommended the retention at least of Meulensteen[174] because he wanted to be his own man.

It was a no-brainer in fact. Against the risk of being undermined he had a ready-made excuse for failure if he had simply followed that advice and, assuming it had worked out as badly as it has, he would probably now be starting on a second year but with all his own square pegs in round holes. He was always going to have his work cut out to persuade the Glazers to curtail the extravagances of their respective lifestyles in order to ensure that the golden goose continued to lay its precious eggs and, if he had summoned up the courage to ask unsuccessfully, the reality is he might not have been long in the job anyway. Once again, damned if you do; damned if you don't.

The upshot of that was the same for the new manager, Louis Van Gaal. If he did not ask, the team might have been doomed to relative anonymity - might still be until the owners wake up and smell the coffee or bale out. If the latter, it will be at substantially less than the sums quoted in Forbes magazine and, whatever the price, it may be that the MEC prediction will come true, if not for the reasons they supposed, that United as a club will be "toxic" for football generations to come. However, LVG seems to be one who will not suffer fools gladly and is unlikely to take any prisoners. He has no reason to over-respect Ferguson's achievements because, even if they are unlikely to be matched to precisely the same degree by any manager in the future, the arenas in which they have met are ones where the newcomer can claim to have at the least held his own[175].

---

174   Eric Steel (goalkeeping coach) in interview with fanzine United We Stand 30th September 2013. Ferguson in his "after-management" interview with Jim Rosenthal on MUTV 2014 has suggested that he recommended Mick Phelan to his successor so this is not entirely without contradiction.

175   The two meetings which really spring to mind are the clashes with Barca in 1999 both of

The achievements are therefore singular but relative.

It is probably axiomatic to say that the background to football now is not as it was prior to the television explosion which was the catalyst of Manchester United's success in that it was the club best placed to take advantage of the boom of the early 90's. This means, however, that it is probably as hard for any of approximately a dozen or so clubs in the world to fall off the radar just as it is for some others to get on it except with some extreme "benevolence" from third parties. Thus, United is not likely to be out of the mix indefinitely but there is no doubt that, with spiralling debt, "hard" does not mean "impossible". Assuming, therefore, that LVG does not reprise some of the success of the Ferguson years within the three years of his contract or, assuming, which is perhaps even more likely, that he does bring a degree of relative success but, because of advancing age and diminishing ambition, is not able to continue beyond his three year tenure and the task then falls upon less capable shoulders, what happens then? Do the Glazers stand or do they bale?

There are supposed bidders in the shape of the organisation known as the Red Knights, a group made up of businessmen who are all United supporters[176], but the Glazers' valuation of the club was sufficiently off-putting to send these good gentlemen back into their boardrooms, no doubt, they would say, to await a better opportunity. However, the feeling persists that, despite the seriousness of some of the participants, the plan was half-baked and they had no real idea of precisely how they would achieve their end or how, if they did so, they would manage the club any better than their predecessors. They all need a return on their money. There is nothing here for MUST and Shareholders United, or not a great deal anyway. The argument might even run that you are better with the devil you know than a committee of new and lesser devils.

It is hard to look so deep into the abyss as to witness the potential destruction of such a great institution, one which dragged itself from

---

which were high scoring draws and the loss on away goals to Bayern in 2010, a game Ferguson was unlucky to lose.

[176] The news first broke on BBC Sport in January 2010 and simmered throughout the next few months until the proposed bid of £1bn was put on hold in June 2010.

the relative obscurity of the first half of its existence to the very top of world football, but the warning signs are there. The giants of yesteryear like Wolves (1950's) and Leeds United (1970's) are languishing in the lower leagues and have known no significant success for many years. In the case of Leeds this fall from grace was precipitated by significant over-borrowing on an unprecedented scale but its debts never exceeded one quarter of those taken on by United in the Glazer takeover, albeit the club is a much smaller animal in this particular financial jungle.[177] It could happen at United and it would not take a massive shift for it to occur, merely a few seasons of mid-table obscurity. Many asked in 2010, after that year's results were published, whether the accumulation of the debt would drag United out of the top tier in the next five years. This was twenty months after the last Champions League triumph and eight months after the club had unsuccessfully gone to a second final in three years. They would go to another in 2011 and this is important because of the revenue it generates. However, that clock is still ticking.[178]

The world of top football is a tiger. Once you have it by the tail you cannot afford to let go. If the Glazers think they can finesse their way through the next five years as they have through the last nine they are going to find themselves faced with the consequences of running their prized asset into the ground or rather into the lower tiers of the league. One would hope that this would be a significant concern to them but they too may have been lulled into a false sense of security by Ferguson's success and may have believed that his successor, precisely because he was the great man's choice, would be equally successful. At least the myth of the invincibility of Sir Alex's judgment has been debunked sooner rather than later and there is, thus, still time to do something about it. Of course there is another viewpoint: the sad reality is that the Glazers may not care as long as they have from the club all that they need by the point of the meltdown.

---

[177] The phrase "doing a Leeds" came to be synonymous with financial mismanagement of football clubs and no doubt has been at the forefront of Arsena'l's thinking when it chose stadium redevelopment over spending on the team building necessary to success.

[178] See e.g The Guardian 12th January 2010.

The 2014-2015 season and the following one should be enough to tell if 2005 was the beginning of the next phase of the club's illustrious history or the watershed which was to the forefront of John Warrington's mind when he posed that question after that year's Cup Final, itself the scene of so much mourning.

CHAPTER 16
REQUIEM OR REINCARNATION

It seems therefore that this is the point where one should begin to draw some conclusions, if not in answer to the question posed by John Warrington ("Does 2005 mark the beginning of the end?"), then at least to the one posed by me which is derived from that ("How did United get to this position in the first place?"). My reasons for United's pre-eminence are a compendium of the following which I have tried to place in chronological order:

1. The emergence of the Busby Babes and the concept of a young, home-grown team which would go on to dominate world football seems to me to begin with Matt Busby and Jimmy Murphy, two men returning from a terrible world war with ambitions to create a peaceful, sporting legacy from all that had gone before. Matt Busby's vision is the paramount reason for the genesis of the Manchester United team ethos.

2. The Munich air crash followed and with it the mythology of "the flowers of Manchester". A grimy, industrial city in the north west of England created a legend that was near Arthurian in its concept. These brave knights go out from Camelot and the Round Table where they engage in jousts with deadly foes until ultimately they die on a foreign battlefield. The concept of the pure, young knight, the Sir Galahad figure, comes alive in the character of Duncan Edwards, probably the greatest player of his generation, a contender (at least in mythological terms) for the greatest player of all time. That is now the template of the team. Whether it would simply become fossilized as most myths do or whether it would grow into a new faith depended on what would happen next.

3. The trinity of Best, Law and Charlton is what happened next and they became synonymous with football excellence – arguably the best front three in the world, supplanting the two of Puskas and Di Stefano. Each of them within a short period of one another won the

accolade of the European Footballer of the Year[179] and each had his adherents claiming him to be the best, or perhaps the most influential, footballer on the planet of his time. The image was amplified by the simultaneous freeing of European culture from the chains and the dogmas of the war years and by the new spirit of optimism, which was abroad. The belief was there, and of course not just in football, that this was a generation which could change the world and all it stood for. United's rise was contemporaneous with the Swinging Sixties,[180] the "white heat of technology" speech,[181] and the emergence of George Best as the first real football celebrity, an icon like the Beatles.

4. There followed the almost magical nature of the European Champions' Cup success at Wembley against Benfica in 1968 and the decade-long vindication (for Busby and the club) of the tragedy of 1958.

These events were enough to sustain the club through one of its most difficult periods in which it saw firstly the usurpation of its throne by Manchester City, a circumstance which is in evidence again in the modern era, albeit on the first occasion it proved to be yet another of those flashes in the pan which has been the hallmark of City's progress down the years. But then it was followed by a much greater threat, the emergence of Bill Shankly's and Bob Paisley's Liverpool, whose period of European dominance coincided with a loss of confidence and a withdrawing into themselves of the great southern football bastions of Spain and Italy and the return into hibernation of the German and Dutch masters of Bayern and Ajax.

5. There was an element then of good fortune in what followed because the communications and proliferation-of-knowledge cultures took off for real at the beginning of the 1990's and Manchester United was poised in exactly the right place at exactly the right time with just enough of its cultural heritage from the Sixties left to take advantage of the new revolution. The wealth of

---

179   Law won the Ballon d'Or in 1964, Charlton in 1966 and Best in 1968.
180   A phrase attributed to Diana Vreeland of Vogue Magazine in the Weekend Telegraph of 16th April 1965. It has its echoes now with "Cool Britannia".
181   Harold Wilson's speech to the Labour Party Conference of 1963.

the club immediately after the flotation on the Stock Market of 1991 meant it could outstrip all of its rivals in spending power except for those who might have "sugar daddy" type benefactors. There were few of these around then because football had not begun to attract the mega-rich of the world as it didn't yet have the media exposure and hype that brings.

The latter could, of course, only compete during the period of the availability of that largesse whereas United was a money-making machine which could go on and on forever or so it seemed piling up the cash and spending it on the team. It was a corporation which knew exactly what its business was, where its market was and it went out to exploit this with almost ruthless efficiency in those early days, leaving its erstwhile rivals standing.

6. The acquisition of the great Frenchman, Eric Cantona, from United's great rivals and the League Champions of the previous year, Leeds United, then captured the public imagination. It was a coup of extraordinary proportions and the Frenchman was indeed the catalyst who changed United from a nearly team to serial winners and he did it with such panache, such Gallic flair and elegance allied to a really tough interior, that the great British public which did not support other teams took to him like a long lost friend. In many ways his finest moment was his kung-fu kick. The press might berate him, the authorities might threaten to lock him up for it, but it was an iconic moment, one when you felt someone did the wrong thing perhaps but for all the right reasons and it couldn't have happened to a nicer victim![182]

7. The emergence then of the great saviour's disciples, the class of 1992, with him as the Arthurian figure, the great egalitarian with his Round Table for his young knights to sit around and carouse, simply put the rightful king back on his throne in Camelot.[183] This team was

---

[182]   This is the famous moment on 25th January 1995 when Eric leapt the retaining wall at Crystal Palace and went into the crowd where he kicked the foul-mouthed racist, Matthew Simmons. An eye-witness account is given on the Republik of Mancunia website by Darren Richman of The Independent.

[183]   There is an iconic picture of Eric posing as a Roman Emperor with his young acolytes at his feet, holding court like some regal Socrates, but I prefer the Celtic tradition for my imagery.

then for the first time since the 1950's a mirror image of the Busby Babes and that simply augmented United's reputation as the team of youth, the team of flair, and brought another seam of gold and another group of gilded boy-knights to add to the mythology of the neo-Arthurian nature of the legend. The young players were like questing knights in their attempt to overcome all odds and conquer Europe. Giggs, Beckham, Scholes, Butt and Neville, not to mention Keane, Irwin, Yorke, Cole and Solskjaer and others, may not qualify as knights-errant like Lancelot, Galahad, Gawain, Perceval, Bors *et al* (and they were in truth as all-too-human as the rest of us) but they certainly carried with them into Europe the spirit of Romance. This culminated, after a number of heady, record-breaking years, in the almost mythical nature of the capture of the European Cup, the Holy Grail, in 1999.[184]

8. Finally, there was the emergence of David Beckham as the most famous football icon of modern times, the epitome of the true, fair and gracious knight, squaring, effectively, the other circle of the celebrity footballer which ran alongside the more whimsical Arthurian one to which I have referred. This circle was of course the one created almost individually by George Best but it is one taken to a new level of perfection by David, who has simultaneously managed to retain a degree of humility, good grace and dignity which has not perhaps always been a character trait of his great ancestor, the Northern Irishman, until the latter's untimely death on 25th November 2005.[185]

9. When it seemed that United had lost that iconic figure to its arch-rival, Real Madrid, who should emerge in his place but that later standard-bearer of the same image, Cristiano Ronaldo? His emergence is the story of someone who can be described beyond any shadow of a doubt as one of the of the two greatest footballers in the world, his ongoing rivalry with Lionel Messi of Barcelona merely

---

184   "God is an Englishman," wrote *L' Equipe*.

185   Best was famous throughout his life for depicting his life (and the squandering of his talents) as one great party and as having no regrets but the *News of the World* (authenticated as might be necessary for that sometimes less than reliable periodical by the fact that it was allowed to take a death-bed photograph of him so he probably remained commercial to the end) reported that his last words were "don't die like me". This suggests a certain amount of repenting at leisure with which many of us can identify.

spicing up the debate even further. Ronaldo and to a lesser extent Rooney carried through and rammed home that same image of Manchester United as the team of flair and of youthful brilliance, which so captured the imagination of the young people of many different cultures world-wide. The light they shed lit up an otherwise drab and ugly world.

10. There is no magic without Merlin. None of the above could have occurred without the wizards - in this case both Sir Matt Busby and then Sir Alex Ferguson. Whatever detractors might have to say, and I have made a number of criticisms myself, the reality is that all these pale into insignificance in comparison with the achievements. Both men were flawed in many ways and it is the result of the increasingly intrusive nature of the twentieth century that more of these are known in Sir Alex's case than are in Sir Matt's but both of them probably had sociopathic tendencies. Their vision counted above all else and no one could deter them. In both cases this could have caused the destruction of the club. They are not alone because these tendencies appear more and more to be the essential ingredient for success in the modern business world.

If there is an eleventh point it has not yet been written or, if it has and I have missed it among the trees, I shall leave it for someone else to add.

So, I come to the end of this quest and I ask, was the requiem the right thing to write about? The answer of course was no, not at least in the short term, because there was life in the club and the force that drives the red fuse was still active in its roots. I have said previously that to some this may be a mere football club but to me it is a creature beyond history. It has passed into myth like the creators of great religions and like those Knights of the Round Table who were the embodiment of the spirit of Romance and of all that was good in the world, in other words the mythical realms of the golden era which have never in fact existed except in the imaginary world of the human spirit.

I couldn't imagine a life without Manchester United but I am forced to contemplate that, without great care and great nurturing, it could come to pass. It has given me a sense of mystery and of the divine and it has given me a sense of fellowship within this tribe of many creeds, colours and backgrounds of people who feel the same sense of devotion. The emotion I have for it cannot be described as anything less than love for an entity which has itself given so much pleasure and hope to me among so many, a creature which to me appears to be alive and to possess a soul, the living embodiment of the people who support it.

It may not be the purest of love, like that of a parent for a child; it may indeed be a burning, selfish, passionate love as for a person whom one wants entirely to oneself. But it is love and I would not expect to hear it described much differently from the fans of other clubs. For our own part we all count ourselves fortunate to be United fans and we hate with a passion anyone who could think of doing any harm to this beautiful creation of God and of men. God forgive that we should wish the darkest possible evil on any who contemplates that, but there is no doubt that we do.

Malcolm Glazer passed away on 28th May 2014. The *Love United Hate Glazer* campaign has never abated during his lifetime. The reaction from United fans, even those who resented the owners unreservedly and without any of the healing usually associated with time, was muted. It was significant perhaps that this controversial owner died at the close of a season and, indeed, of the poorest season that United had endured for nearly three decades, because, if the news had come to a packed stadium during that season, it is shameful perhaps but desperately doubtful that there would have been a fully observed minute's silence or indeed, as seems to be the modern approach, a uniform expression of respect in a minute's applause. Perhaps this isn't strange in light of the fact that he never once visited the club. The paraphrasing of John Kennedy's famous speech[186] is apposite in the sense that there is no evidence that Mr. Glazer was ever interested in what he might do for Manchester United but only in what it could do for him and his extended family. [187] It did much for them, tripling or even quadrupling their net worth[188]

---

186   JFK Inauguration speech - Washington 20th January 1961.
187   Jim White Telegraph 29th May 2014.

at the expense of the club's investment in its own playing infrastructure. MUST stated in response to the dismissal of David Moyes as club manager that: *"In short the sooner the Glazers recognise that Manchester United has to be able to reinvest its own revenues, and that there will be no surplus for them to cream off, the sooner they'll realise they need to cut and run before the market corrects the vastly inflated valuation of Manchester United. This is based on profits that cannot be sustained if the re-investment necessary to compete is to be made"*.[189]

The doom and gloom scaremongering of this forecast, i.e. the suggestion that the only salvation is for the Glazers to quit the club, is hyperbole of the type in which the self-named Manchester United's Supporters Trust often indulges itself, probably as a means of getting its message across in circumstances where it is allowed no official consultative voice in the running of the club, which has an entirely different and tamer supporter's representation.[190] Of course it could be corrected from within by a different business approach but there must be genuine fear that this can never be generated in a family which is only concerned about its own wealth.

If United does not return to the top or somewhere within striking distance of the top of the tree by the close of season 2015-2016 there is a risk that the decline could be terminal and will only be arrested once football ceases to be such a financially lucrative business and, therefore, returns to its grass roots. That will probably take at least a generation to happen. It probably will happen if only because the current global football business model is unsustainable. Fans cannot continue to pay the ludicrously high prices to support the lifestyles of football celebrities; clubs cannot continue to be indebted to the point of extinction; income cannot continue to be taken out of the clubs to support the lifestyles of stakeholders. The whole circus of celebrity sport has echoes of the Colosseum or some other Roman arena where the games are held regularly to keep the mob (as the common people were known) distracted and therefore under control.

188	USD4.5bn at the time of his death. Forbes 7th June 2014.
189	Extract from MUST press release of 22nd April 2014.
190	The official Manchester United Supporters Club.

Sooner or later something has to give.

Ticket prices in Germany are less than half the price of those in England and Wales. Barcelona with revenues of £407m was the highest earner of the 2012 - 2013 season and the average price of a season ticket was £172. Manchester United earned £331.4m but the average season ticket cost £532. Bayern Munich earned £290.3m and its average season ticket cost £67.[191] There is little doubt about which way is the best to go. In Germany there is a 50%+1 rule where commercial interests are not allowed to gain control of a club and it must remain owned by the members. Audi and Adidas own stakes in the German club but less than 20% between them. The rest is controlled by the club's members.[192] The only exceptions are Wolfsburg and Leverkusen which started as works teams and are owned by Volkswagen and Bayer respectively.

The Germans would not permit foreign billionaires such as Glazer, Abramovich or Sheikh Mansour to take control of its top clubs. Its capitalism is every bit as committed as the US/UK model but tends to be more interventionist in common with German tradition. Thus, the government would intervene because it would perceive the existence of a threat to a significant proportion of the population. In the UK at the time of the Glazer takeover the government perception was that it could not intervene despite the wish of many ministers, apparently, to do so.[193] Moreover, notwithstanding the call for "a political economy of football" in articles since[194] there has been very little progress to prevent this from ever happening again.

Indeed it was odd to see the Labour government of the time of the Glazer takeover deciding it couldn't intervene. Constitutional Affairs Minister Harriet Harman did claim that her government had urged the Glazers to engage constructively with fans, the FA and the club.

---

[191] BBC News Berlin 24th May 2013 (just before the Munich v Dortmund ECL Final at Wembley).
[192] The German model isn't perfect, though, in the sense that it is very largely a one club state where Bayern simply acquires its rivals best players in order to sustain its own hegemony.
[193] Patrick Hennessy Telegraph 15th May 2005.
[194] See for example that The University of Warwick in 2007 entitled *An Analytical Framework For A Political Economy of Football*.

"Manchester United is very important to English football and the government is keeping a very close eye on the situation".[195] One takes that with a pinch of salt, of course, but it is worthy of the observation that the Seeing Eye is nothing without the hand to act. In truth this was just a piece of pure hypocrisy and there is no reason to believe that the government was concerned at all. Tony Blair knew Ferguson quite well. At the unveiling of the manager's statue in 2012 he praised him in words normally used of warriors as "a leader of people". Slightly more disingenuously he also praised his "huge integrity to himself and to what he believes in" which sounds as if the former Prime Minister could then have been speaking of himself.[196] It is a pity perhaps that seven years or so earlier he did not feel able to intervene.[197] He did in just about everything else - but perhaps that was where American interests were engaged on the same side, if that is not too unkind. Blair was very good at making it up as he went along. It would have been easy for him at that point to step into the commercial arena and actually stop it from happening, just as he had stepped, with that belief in his own omniscience, into just about every other arena. If he was such a great friend of Ferguson's then it is perhaps odd that he didn't do more. Some would say that it would have been a terrible day for democracy if he had, but in fact it wouldn't have been that at all. It would have been just another day of Blair reinvention of the rules and on this occasion he would have earned the gratitude of millions and would at least have had a bolt-hole in Manchester (Cheshire perhaps) when all the rest of the nation came to revile him.[198]

However, this is all for the future and, if I were going to gamble on potential outcomes, I would expect the United phoenix to rise again within 2 or 3 years, even though there is no doubt that the burden of

---

195   BBC News 12th May 2005.
196   Mancunian Matters 22nd November 2012.
197   Blair became PM on 2nd May 1997 and vacated the office on 27th June 2007.
198   Of course he didn't need it because he couldn't wait to cross benches towards the "capitalist" side. He is reputed to have earned £80m since leaving office although no one is certain of precisely what for. He has been an adviser to various banking institutions but couldn't prevent the banking crisis of 2008, which he helped to create; he has also been a Middle East Peace Envoy as well and that has worked out well. See This Is Money 2nd July 2012. In short, it would not be unfair to take the view that he is a betrayer rather than the saviour he purported to be and that his feet of clay are there for all to observe.

the debt is a significant one. Whether it is as great a burden as that which United overcame after the war, or as that it overcame after Munich, or even as that it overcame after the Liverpool dominance of the upper echelons of English football between 1970 and 1990, is yet to be seen. Macro-economics will have an effect on that and Manchester United's fortunes will be tied up with those of the rest of the world. Confidently, though, I would gamble on a good outcome.

Bringing Home the Bodies (1958)

One could of course come back to these words in ten years' time and wonder, how did I write that? How could I get it so spectacularly wrong? There are no doubt many out there who are willing that to happen just as there are many who are willing that it won't. Hence, one comes back to the strength of an institution and its long-term rather than short-term health and, takes account of how the institution has survived this crisis so far,[199] as well as those which have gone before it, and the fact that each time it has come back

---

[199] Crisis, what crisis, one might be forgiven for saying. One ECL and two more losing finals and five EPLs is arguably the club's most successful period ever whilst carrying the debt burden.

stronger and fitter. Therefore, looking, in a word, at everything, my conclusion is that the ill-wishers will be disappointed yet again and Manchester United will bounce back and may be bigger and stronger than ever. The club is harder to kill than the salamander fish.

My answer to John's question, therefore, the one posed in Cardiff as long ago as 21st May 2005 and which I am profoundly sorry to have taken so long to get to, is that everything goes in cycles but I would expect this trough to be a relatively shallow one. To paraphrase the late Sir Matt: no it is not the end; it is just another beginning.[200]

50 years after Munich (Moscow 2008)

---

200   Believed to be from Sir Matt Busby's speech on his acceptance of the freedom of the City of Manchester.

Cristian Ronaldo and Wes Brown Champions League Final held at Luzhniki Stadium Moscow 21 May 2008 and contested by Manchester United v Chelsea
Mitch Gunn / Shutterstock.com

THANK YOU TO ALL THE FANS OF THE BEAUTIFUL GAME WHO PURCHASED MY BOOK. I WOULD LOVE TO HEAR FEEDBACK, SO PLEASE LEAVE A REVIEW.

HERE IS TO MANCHESTER UNITED THE 2015 SEASON and THE FUTURE.

*Man U Stadium credit - **naipung / Shutterstock.com***

Printed in Great Britain
by Amazon.co.uk, Ltd.,
Marston Gate.